**INVESTIGATING
DISEASES**

Investigating
Eating Disorders (Anorexia,
Bulimia, and Binge Eating):
Real Facts for Real Lives

Library of Congress Cataloguing-in-Publication Data

Ambrose, Marylou.
   Investigating eating disorders (anorexia, bulimia, and binge eating): real facts for
   real lives / Marylou Ambrose and Veronica Deisler.
      p. cm.—(Investigating diseases)
   Includes bibliographical references and index.
   Summary: "Provides information about eating disorders, including
   treatment, diagnosis, history, medical advances, and true stories about people
   with the diseases"—Provided by publisher.
   ISBN-978-0-7660-3339-9
   1. Anorexia nervosa—Juvenile literature. 2. Bulimia—Juvenile literature.
   I. Deisler, Veronica. II. Title.
   RC552.A5A43 2011
   616.85'262—dc22

                                                  2009006492

Printed in the United States of America

022010 Lake Book Manufacturing, Inc., Melrose Park, IL

10 9 8 7 6 5 4 3 2 1

To Our Readers:
We have done our best to make sure all Internet Addresses in this book were active and appropriate when we went to press. However, the author and the publisher have no control over and assume no liability for the material available on those Internet sites or on other Web sites they may link to. Any comments or suggestions can be sent by e-mail to comments@enslow.com or to the address on the back cover.

♻ Enslow Publishers, Inc., is committed to printing our books on recycled paper. The paper in every book contains 10% to 30% post-consumer waste (PCW). The cover board on the outside of each book contains 100% PCW. Our goal is to do our part to help young people and the environment too!

Photo Credits: © Alfred Pasieka/Photo Researchers, p. 92; AP Photo/Eugenio Savio, p. 26; AP Photo/Peter Kramer, pp. 11 (Sigler), 25 (Winfrey); © Doctor Stock, p. 33; © iStock/Aldo Murillo, p. 129; © iStock/Alexander Hafemann, p. 114; © iStock/Asli Cetin, p. 38; © iStock/Bart Coenders, p. 81; © iStock/Bill Grove, p. 60; © iStock/blaneyphoto, p. 28; © iStock/bluestocking, p. 94; © iStock/Brian Moore, p. 90; © iStock/Catherine Yeulet, pp. 7, 56, 86; © iStock/Chris Schmidt, p. 121; © iStock/Claude Dagenais, p. 61; © iStock/Elke Dennis, p. 32; © iStock/Galina Barskaya, p. 22; © iStock/Igor Stepovik, p. 41; © iStock/Jacom Stephens, p. 65; © iStock/Jason Woodcock, p. 116; © iStock/Jennifer Trenchard, p. 124; © iStock/Jim Jurica, p. 132; © iStock/Juan Monino, p. 34; © iStock/Julie de Leseleuc, p. 11 (phone); © iStock/kkgas, p. 103; © iStock/Lisa Klumpp, p. 105; © iStock/mandygodbehear, p. 130; © iStock/Marcin Balcerzak, p. 80; © iStock/Mike Drayton, p. 18; © iStock/Reuben Schulz, p. 16; © iStock/Ron Sumners, p. 36; © iStock/Sean Locke, p. 85; © iStock/Simon Matthews, p. 77; © iStock/Stockphoto4u, p. 4; © iStock/Tony Sanchez, p. 72; © iStock/TravelPixPro, p. 3; © iStock/Tyler Stalman, p. 20; © iStock/Westbury, p. 45; © Michael Ochs Archives/Getty Images, p. 44; © Shutterstock, p. 134; © Stock Exchange, pp. 31, 96; © Stock Exchange/Karen Barefoot, p. 74; © Stock Exchange/linusb4, p. 111; © Stock Exchange/yenhoon, p. 122; USDA, p. 63; © Wenn/Newscom, p. 25 (Clarkson); Wikimedia Commons, pp. 46, 47, 50.

Cover Photos: © iStock/TravelPixPro

INVESTIGATING
DISEASES

Investigating
Eating Disorders (Anorexia, Bulimia, and Binge Eating):
Real Facts for Real Lives

**Marylou Ambrose
and
Veronica Deisler**

Enslow Publishers, Inc.
40 Industrial Road
Box 398
Berkeley Heights, NJ 07922
USA

Table of Contents

What Are Eating Disorders?

An eating disorder is a psychological illness characterized by a severe disturbance in eating behavior. The most common are anorexia nervosa, bulimia nervosa, and binge-eating disorder.

WHAT ARE THE SYMPTOMS?

Symptoms of anorexia are extreme thinness, fear of weight gain, fasting, unrealistic body image, loss of menstruation, and purging techniques, such as self-induced vomiting and misuse of laxatives. Symptoms of bulimia are binge eating, unrealistic body image, self-induced vomiting, misuse of laxatives, and excessive exercise. One symptom of binge-eating disorder is eating large amounts of food rapidly until feeling uncomfortably full. Binge-eating disorder does not include purging, fasting, or excessive exercise.

WHAT CAUSES EATING DISORDERS?

The causes of eating disorders are complex. It is believed they result from a combination of biology (genes and brain chemicals), psychology (depression and anxiety), emotions (low self-esteem and perfectionism), and culture (pressure from society to be thin).

HOW MANY PEOPLE HAVE EATING DISORDERS?

An estimated 10 million women and 1 million men in the United States have anorexia or bulimia. Millions more suffer from binge-eating disorder, the most common eating disorder in the United States today.

WHO GETS EATING DISORDERS?

Anybody can get an eating disorder, but they are most often found among young women ages twelve to twenty-five. Dieting is the most common risk factor for developing an eating disorder.

ARE THEY TREATABLE?

Although people with eating disorders can never be fully cured, if treated by professionals, they can live full and rewarding lives.

ARE THEY PREVENTABLE?

There is no simple way to prevent eating disorders. Learning more about them is a good place to start. Building a positive self-image, expressing feelings, and living a healthy lifestyle also help.

Introduction

Everyone has heard of eating disorders. Television, magazines, tabloids, and the Internet keep readers and viewers up to date on which celebrities look too thin on the red carpet or too fat on the beach. But how much do people really understand about these illnesses?

The answer is: *not enough*. Eating disorders are not just about eating too little or too much. They are serious psychological illnesses. They affect as many as 24 million American males and females of all ages, races, and ethnic groups.

Unfortunately, most people who starve themselves, gorge themselves, or vomit after eating never go for treatment because they are too scared and ashamed. This keeps eating disorders veiled in secrecy. Researchers are still unlocking the mysteries of these complex diseases, but much more work needs to be done.

People with eating disorders need months or years of professional treatment to get better. They almost never recover on their own. Those who do not get help can end up with permanent medical problems. They can even die. Going for treatment early is critical.

This book covers the three major eating disorders, anorexia nervosa, bulimia nervosa, and binge-eating disorder, as well as some less common eating disorders. It describes causes and symptoms, diagnosis and treatment, risk factors and prevention, and promising research. You will also read inspiring stories of real people who have overcome their eating disorders and gone on to lead healthy, productive lives.

CHAPTER ONE

Straight Talk About Eating Disorders

A STAR WITH A SECRET

Jamie-Lynn Sigler had everything going for her. At age sixteen, the Long Island, New York, high school junior got a starring role as Meadow, the head mobster's daughter, on the HBO television series *The Sopranos*. But between filming the pilot in 1997 and filming the show's first season a year later, something happened that almost cost Jamie-Lynn her acting career—and her life.

It all started when her boyfriend broke up with her. Devastated, she began to wonder if there was something wrong with the way she looked. Was she too fat at 120 pounds? She decided to use diet and exercise to improve her appearance.

Jamie-Lynn started skipping desserts and walking on a treadmill for twenty minutes before school. She lost a few pounds and was happy, so she took her diet and exercise program to the next level—and the next, and the next. Pretty soon she was getting up at 3 A.M. and exercising for four hours before school, taking seven dance classes a week, and eating only about 400 calories a day.

"I would constantly make excuses that I ate already, or I wasn't hungry, or I was rushing here or there," she remembered.[1]

Continued on next page

Jamie-Lynn Sigler, of *Sopranos* fame, battled an eating disorder for many years.

Continued from previous page

In four months, Jamie-Lynn lost forty pounds.

"I was wearing basically children's clothes. It was hard to find clothes that would fit," she said. "Every week . . . I would see more bones coming out, more ribs, and more hip bones. It was awful."[2]

Although Jamie-Lynn wanted to go out for pizza with her friends, have sleepovers, and do the things other teenagers do, she couldn't. Counting calories and exercising had taken over her life.

"I truly lost [the] will to live," she said. "I seriously contemplated suicide because I felt that no one in this world would ever understand the constant battle I had in my head every day."[3]

At her lowest weight, Jamie-Lynn weighed eighty pounds. Her parents begged her to eat more and exercise less, but she ignored them. Then one day, riding in the car during a family trip, Jamie-Lynn fell apart. Her rigid diet and exercise regimen had been disrupted and she couldn't handle it. She began crying and shaking and finally confessed: "I have an eating disorder. I want help."[4]

The next day, her parents took her to a nutritionist, who counseled her on proper nutrition, and to a therapist who helped her understand the reasons for her eating disorder. The therapist also put her on Prozac, a drug that is often prescribed to control the depressed feelings that occur in people with eating disorders.

Jamie-Lynn had anorexia nervosa and she was also a compulsive exerciser. People with anorexia virtually stop eating. Those who exercise compulsively try to get rid of any calories they do eat by working out for hours every day.

In a month, Jamie-Lynn had gained back five pounds and was on her way to recovery. But when she arrived on the set to film the first season of *The Sopranos*, the other actors were shocked. She did not look like the girl they had met a year before—she was thirty-five pounds thinner.

"I remember [actor] Jim Gandolfini took my arm and wrapped his whole hand around it," Jamie-Lynn said. "And he was like, 'Are you eating?'"[5]

The show's producers were concerned that she looked too thin for the part and might not have the stamina to do the job. So they started auditioning other actresses.

Ultimately, the producers decided to stick with Jamie-Lynn, who promised to gain back all the weight she had lost. Eight months later, when *The Sopranos* began its second season, Jamie-Lynn was back up to 120 pounds and looked and felt healthy again.

After that, she opened up to her fellow cast members about her eating disorder. She also began talking about her eating disorder on an HBO fan Web site and speaking about them on television and in magazines. She even wrote a book called *Wise Girl: What I've Learned about Life, Love, and Loss*, which tells the story of her life, including her battle with anorexia and compulsive exercising. Today, Jamie-Lynn is a spokesperson for the National Eating Disorders Association (NEDA), encouraging young people to have healthy body images and teaching the public about eating disorders.

Jamie-Lynn played Meadow Soprano for six years, until the award-winning show ended in 2006. She has also acted in movies and on the Broadway stage. Her career, life, and health are back on track. But even though she is healthy now, she still lives in the shadow of her eating disorders every day.

"With eating disorders, they're like any addiction," she said. "There's always the possibility of a fallback, with an emotional setback or whatever. But now I have the tools to be more aware."[6]

For this reason, she carries in her purse a photo of herself at eighty pounds, as a reminder of what she has conquered and what might possibly happen again.[7]

The tools people with eating disorders need to stay healthy include the following:

- support from family and friends
- professional help from nutritionists and therapists, and
- information from organizations like the NEDA.

Most people cannot win the battle against eating disorders alone. Eating disorders can take over a person's life in only a few weeks, and life-threatening weight loss can occur in a few months. Without treatment, people may suffer permanent damage to body organs, including the brain; lose bone strength; or even die.

"The biggest step is admitting you have a problem," Jamie-Lynn said.[8] Once people get past this hurdle, they can start re-learning good eating and exercise habits. They can stop feeling hopeless. They can get healthy and start living normal lives again.

"I thought that was my life. I was set. This was the way I was going to have to live my life," Jamie-Lynn said. "And knowing that I was able to overcome it and be healthy and happy again is amazing."[9]

WHAT IS AN EATING DISORDER?

An eating disorder is a psychological (mental) illness. It starts in the mind, but it can have devastating effects on the body. Some people, like Jamie-Lynn Sigler, are obsessed with being thin and diet and exercise excessively. At the opposite extreme are those who eat too much and cannot stop. Whether overeating or starving themselves, all those who suffer from eating disorders have an abnormal, unhealthy relationship with food.

This love-hate relationship with food takes many forms. People with eating disorders may go several days without eating, eat only a few foods, make themselves vomit after eating, or eat until they are stuffed. They may also exercise excessively.

What Is Obesity?

Obese people just weigh too much, right? Well, yes and no. Overweight and obesity are not just measured in pounds. Both also depend on a person's age and body mass index (BMI).

Body mass index is the most accurate measure of understanding whether a person is overweight or obese. It is easy to calculate using a person's weight and height. To calculate BMI for adults, divide weight (in pounds) by height (in inches squared) and then multiply by 703.

Once a BMI is calculated, it is checked against the following table:

BMI Weight	Status
Below 18.5	Underweight
18.5 – 24.9	Normal
25.0 – 29.9	Overweight
30.0 and above	Obese[10]

Body mass index is calculated the same way for children and teens, but instead of the table above, percentile charts are used. Boys and girls have different amounts of body fat, so they have separate charts. Percentiles range from zero to one hundred. Young people whose BMIs hover around the fiftieth percentile have an average BMI, but those with BMIs in low percentiles are considered underweight. Those with BMIs in high percentiles are considered overweight.

Body mass calculators can be found on the Internet. But the most accurate way for a teen to find out his or her percentile is to be weighed in a doctor's office or by a school nurse. Also, keep in mind that athletes, bodybuilders, and other muscular people may have high BMIs, but this is due to increased muscle mass, not fat.

These behaviors can damage the heart, muscles, bones, and many other parts of the body. Also, because such behaviors are time-consuming and done in secret, they harm friendships, family relationships, work, and school work.

People suffering from eating disorders do not usually talk about them. They know that starving themselves, stuffing themselves, making themselves throw up, or exercising until they almost drop are not healthy behaviors. So they hide these behaviors, out of embarrassment and shame. Consequently, many people live with eating disorders for months or years, while their health deteriorates and their personal relationships fall apart.

To make matters worse, eating disorders are not always easy to recognize. If a person is emaciated (extremely thin) or obese (extremely overweight), friends or family members may suspect an eating disorder. But some people who have eating disorders are of normal weight. Even doctors can have trouble identifying them. Patients may complain of problems brought on by their eating disorder (like depression), so doctors treat these problems without knowing their real causes.

For example, in a recent study of adults with eating disorders, more than half said they had asked their doctors for help with a psychological problem. But less than half said they had asked their doctors for help with their eating disorder.[11]

Eating disorders do not just run their course like a cold or the flu. Jamie-Lynn Sigler needed professional help to overcome her problems, and so do most people. She said eating disorders are like an addiction, and some experts agree. They believe that

People who suffer from eating disorders often hide them, but complain about feeling depressed and exhausted, when it is actually their eating disorder that causes the depression and exhaustion.

people with eating disorders can get healthy again, but are never actually cured. Like alcoholics or drug addicts, people who suffer from eating disorders get better, but are always in the recovery stage.

To recover, people with eating disorders must totally change the way they think about food and their bodies. This is hard, but it can be achieved with professional help and the support of family and friends.

Carolyn Costin, author of books on eating disorders and director of several treatment facilities, disagrees. A former anorexia sufferer, she believes that people can make full recoveries and learn to relate to food in a healthy way. She says: "Drug addicts and alcoholics don't have to learn how to control the consumption of drugs or alcohol. (But) a person with an eating disorder has to deal with food every day."[12]

To recover, people with eating disorders must totally change the way they think about food and their bodies. This is hard, but it can be achieved with professional help and the support of family and friends.

TYPES OF EATING DISORDERS

The most common eating disorders are anorexia nervosa, bulimia nervosa, binge-eating disorder, and eating disorders not otherwise specified (EDNOS). This last category includes disorders that are very similar to anorexia and bulimia, but do not meet the diagnostic criteria.

Individuals suffering from anorexia might eat next to nothing at any given meal.

Anorexia and bulimia occur in those who are obsessed with being thin. People with anorexia become extremely thin because they eat next to nothing. People with bulimia may be thin, of normal weight, or slightly overweight; after they eat, they get rid of the food by vomiting or other methods. Some use laxatives. Binge eaters consume huge amounts of food on a regular basis. Most of them are overweight or obese. People with EDNOS have some but not all of the symptoms of anorexia or bulimia.

A national study by Harvard Medical School and McLean Hospital found that during their lifetimes, about 0.9 percent of females and 0.3 percent of males will suffer from anorexia.

fact OR fiction

Older People Do Not Get Eating Disorders

Wrong! People of all ages suffer from eating disorders. Few older men have eating disorders, but they are on the rise in older women. Carolyn Costin, director of the Monte Nido Eating Disorder Treatment Center in California, says: "I used to have mothers calling me about treatment for their daughters; now I get calls from daughters seeking treatment for their mothers."[13]

Costin reported that treatment programs all over the country are seeing more women in their thirties, forties, and fifties. Why? Because older women are not satisfied with their bodies, either. In a recent study of 475 Austrian women aged 60 to 70, about 90 percent said they felt fat. Eighteen women definitely had eating disorders, and another twenty-one reported one symptom of an eating disorder, such as binge eating or vomiting after eating.[14]

In addition, about 1.5 percent of females and 0.5 percent of males will have bulimia, and about 3.5 percent of females and 2 percent of males will have binge-eating disorder.[15] These numbers may actually be higher because many people never receive treatment.

WHO GETS EATING DISORDERS?

Finding reliable statistics on the number of people with eating disorders is difficult. The U.S. government does not track cases of eating disorders as closely as it does cases of other types of diseases. Therefore, experts can only estimate how many people have eating disorders by looking at different research studies.

Eating disorders usually start appearing in the preteen, teen, or young adult years, but in rare cases may appear in children as young as five years old.

Unfortunately, many studies are limited because they are done on only a few hundred people, so they do not show the true extent of the problem. In addition, many researchers only study people being treated for eating disorders. Estimates are probably low because most people never go to a doctor for treatment.[16, 17]

According to the NEDA, about 10 million women and 1 million men in the United States have anorexia or bulimia, and millions more have binge-eating disorder.[18] But the actual number is probably much higher. The Renfrew Center Foundation for Eating Disorders combined U.S. Census Bureau and National Institute of Mental Health statistics and came up with 24 million people with the three most common eating disorders.[19]

Eating disorders usually start appearing in the preteen, teen, or young adult years, but in rare cases may appear in children as young as five years old. Ten times more females than males get eating disorders.[20]

Although men and boys are not as apt to have anorexia or bulimia as women, they are prone to binge eating. The National Institute of Mental Health (NIMH) reports that more than one-third of those with binge-eating disorder are men.[21]

WHO IS AT RISK?

People of all ages, races, and ethnic groups, and both genders, get eating disorders. However, some people are more vulnerable than others. They have certain characteristics—called risk factors—that increase their chances of developing an eating disorder. Here are some major risk factors:

- Being between ages twelve and twenty-five
- Being female
- Living in a family where there is pressure to be thin; overly critical or overprotective parents; or homes where parents abuse alcohol or drugs
- Being a perfectionist or high achiever; having poor self-esteem; a fear of change; or trouble coping with stress
- Undergoing stressful life events, such as leaving for college, getting a new job, losing friends, or breaking up with a girlfriend or boyfriend
- Having a job or taking part in a sport that requires a trim body, such as being an athlete, actor, dancer, or model
- Having another psychological disorder, such as depression or anxiety
- Dieting

Although many teens who are involved in sports are healthy, they are at a higher risk for developing an eating disorder.

- Being overweight
- Being sexually abused in childhood
- Having a close relative with an eating disorder[22]

WHY ARE EATING DISORDERS SO COMMON?

One does not have to be an expert on eating disorders to figure out why they are so common. Today, people are assaulted with images from the media emphasizing that "thin is in." Watching the Victoria's Secret fashion show or looking at the *Sports Illustrated* swimsuit issue is enough to make any girl or woman worry about being thin, never mind putting on a bathing suit. Reading fitness magazines featuring buff bodies and articles called "Lose Your Gut!" or "Flat Belly Diet" can make boys and men feel inadequate.

At the same time, fast-food restaurants are multiplying along with TV commercials for junk foods, and magazines run photos of chocolate cakes next to articles on the latest diets. Talk about mixed signals! It's no wonder eating disorders are on the rise.

WORLDWIDE PROBLEM

As many as 70 million people around the world suffer from eating disorders. In Argentina, eating disorders are about three times as common as in the United States. In Chile, an estimated 70,000 women aged fourteen to thirty have anorexia and 350,000 others have bulimia. Eating disorders are common in Japan, China, and many other parts of the world. Unfortunately, many countries have few or no treatment centers for eating disorders.[23]

TEENS AND EATING DISORDERS

Teens are especially prone to eating disorders. Why? For one thing, they are preoccupied with their bodies, which are growing and changing. Girls whose bodies mature faster than

What Are Incidence and Prevalence?

When researching eating disorders, you may come across the terms *incidence* and *prevalence*. Researchers use the terms *incidence* and *prevalence* to describe how common diseases are. In eating disorders, prevalence describes the estimated number of people in a certain group (such as men, women, or teenagers) who have eating disorders during a certain time period. Incidence describes the number of new cases diagnosed every year.

their friends' may feel so self-conscious, they try to stop the development of normal body fat by dieting.

Teens also have a lot of stress in their lives. They worry about their grades, being popular, doing well in sports, and being attractive. Stress is a part of life, and people of all ages experience it. But teens are still learning how to cope with stress, and might not handle it well.

Teens stress out about taking the SATs, breaking up with their boyfriend or girlfriend, moving to a new town and new school, their parents getting a divorce, abuse, losing friends, and so on. Events they do not have control over are especially stressful. Some teens develop eating disorders because they feel their weight and how much food they eat are the only things in life they *can* control. Ironically, the eating disorder soon creates even more stress and can spiral out of control. For many, the disorder completely takes over their lives.

Gymnasts are at high risk for eating disorders due to the weight restrictions of the sport.

Another pathway to eating disorders includes participating in sports like wrestling, cheerleading, gymnastics, and ice skating. These sports in particular require athletes to be thin, not just fit and healthy. Wrestling is especially troublesome, because athletes must keep their weight within a narrow range to participate. Teens who take part in these sports often diet to keep their weight down, and their dieting can go too far.

Some teens develop eating disorders because they feel their weight and how much food they eat are the only things in life they can control.

EFFECTS OF UNTREATED EATING DISORDERS

An eating disorder that goes untreated can have devastating effects on the body. Getting treatment early can prevent permanent damage. Anorexia can cause a wide range of problems, from frequent bouts of the flu to life-threatening conditions like heart attacks and kidney damage. A few complications of bulimia include tooth decay from constant vomiting, stomach pain, and damage to the stomach and esophagus (the tube that connects the throat with the stomach). Binge-eating disorder can cause obesity, which in turn causes high blood pressure, heart disease, diabetes, and other problems.

Eating disorders also affect the mind. About 50 percent of all people with anorexia, bulimia, and binge-eating disorder suffer from depression (severe sadness and feelings of worthlessness and hopelessness). Depression can cause physical symptoms, too, such as sleeping too much or too little or having trouble concentrating. The depression is usually caused by the eating disorder, but people who are already depressed are more likely to get an eating disorder.[24]

Finally, eating disorders often cause people to withdraw from friends and family, avoid social situations where food is served, lose interest in hobbies, have trouble concentrating, and become moody and irritable.

LIVING WITH EATING DISORDERS

Admitting one has an eating disorder may be the first step to recovery. But afterward, the road can be long and difficult. It can take months or years for people with eating disorders to become healthy again, and not everyone makes a full recovery. Some people revert to old behaviors and need more treatment; others have permanent medical conditions. The key is early recognition and treatment, as well as the support of family and friends. With these tools, people can overcome eating disorders and reclaim their lives and their health.

SAY what

What Is a Psychological Illness?

A psychological (mental) illness disrupts the normal functioning of the mind. It may make people think, feel, and behave in ways that can harm them. People with eating disorders may starve themselves, gorge themselves, and make themselves vomit, or exercise excessively.

CELEBRITIES WHO HAVE SPOKEN PUBLICLY ABOUT THEIR EATING DISORDERS [25, 26, 27]

NAME	OCCUPATION
Paula Abdul	Singer, *American Idol* judge
Victoria Beckham	Member of Spice Girls
Diana	Princess of Wales
Janet Jackson	Singer
Kelly Clarkson	Singer, songwriter
Oprah Winfrey	Talk-show host
Elton John	Singer, songwriter
Amy Winehouse	Singer, songwriter
Cathy Rigby	Olympic gymnast, actress
Nancy Kerrigan	Olympic figure skater

CHAPTER TWO

The Science of Eating Disorders

Twenty-one-year-old runway model Ana Carolina Reston died of complications from anorexia in 2006.

People have been suffering from eating disorders for centuries. But scientists did not recognize the severity of these disorders until the 1970s, when the first major research on anorexia nervosa and bulimia nervosa was published. Eating disorders were not officially classified as mental illnesses until 1980.[1]

Then in 1981, a TV movie called *The Best Little Girl in the World* brought anorexia into American living rooms. When singer Karen Carpenter died from complications of anorexia in 1985, "eating disorder" became a familiar term. (See Chapter 3 for more information.)

Today, images of spindly models and gaunt movie stars are everywhere. The media loves to ask, "Does Mary Kate (or Angelina, or Nicole) have an eating disorder?" Several celebrities have talked openly about their battles with eating disorders. These disorders are big news now, but how much do people really understand about them?

This chapter describes the most common eating disorders: anorexia nervosa, bulimia nervosa, binge-eating disorder, and eating disorders not otherwise specified (EDNOS). It includes why people get the disorders, what signs and symptoms occur, what complications are possible, and more. Prevention, diagnosis, and treatment are covered in Chapters 4 and 5.

ANOREXIA NERVOSA

People with anorexia nervosa are obsessed with being thin. Terrified of gaining weight, they consume very little food and sometimes count every calorie. If they gain weight, they may feel worthless, and when they look in the mirror, they may see a fat person, no matter how thin they really are.

Anorexia is the most deadly of all eating disorders and the hardest to recover from. It is also the most deadly psychiatric disorder. The least common eating disorder, anorexia affects less than one percent of all Americans, or 5 to 10 people in every 100,000.[2] It occurs more often in teenage girls than in any other segment of the population. According to the American Psychiatric Association, one in every one hundred girls and young women has the disorder.[3] Boys, men, and older women do not get anorexia as often, but their numbers are increasing along with society's passion for thinness.

Between 5 and 20 percent of people with anorexia will die from complications of the disease, especially if they have had it a long time. Anorexia has one of the highest death rates of any psychological disorder.[4]

Not everyone who diets develops anorexia, but people who do develop it almost always start by dieting. Then the diet gets out of hand. The most obvious outward sign of anorexia is severe weight loss. People with anorexia weigh at least 15 percent less than what doctors consider normal for their age and height.[5] For example, the average, healthy weight for a 5-foot-4-inch, 16-year-old girl is 115 to 120 pounds.[6] But a girl with anorexia weighs at least 15 percent less—only 98 to 102 pounds—and sometimes much less than that.

If anorexia is allowed to progress, other signs and symptoms besides weight loss occur. These include weakness, exhaustion, faintness, scalp hair loss or thinning, brittle nails, dry skin, swollen hands and feet, purple discoloration on the arms and legs (from decreased blood flow), low blood pressure, slow heartbeat,

When a person suffering from anorexia looks in the mirror, she may see a heavy person, even if she is thin.

coldness, amenorrhea (absence of menstrual periods) in women, low testosterone (male hormone) levels in men, constipation, loss of bone density (osteoporosis), trouble concentrating, and irritability.

As starvation progresses, downy hair called lanugo grows on the arms and stomach. It is the body's way of trying to insulate itself from the cold when the loss of fat and lack of calories make it unable to produce enough heat. In severe anorexia, fluid collects in the brain and brain mass decreases. Finally, the body starts to consume its own fat, tissues, and organs for food. This causes the heart, lungs, and other vital organs to shrink and gradually fail, leading to death.

Like all eating disorders, anorexia involves the mind as well as the body. What begins harmlessly with the desire to lose a few pounds soon spirals out of control. Actually, control is often a key issue in eating disorders. In anorexia, people commonly deny themselves food because what they eat and how much they weigh are things they have power over when the rest of their life seems out of control. They may be scared to death of consuming more than a few calories, fearing they will not be able to stop eating once they start.

People suffering from anorexia have other abnormal ways of thinking and acting. They starve themselves, but they cannot get their minds off food, often cooking for other people and reading cookbooks. At first, they may divide foods into good versus bad or fattening versus nonfattening, but eventually *all* foods become bad and fattening. Finally, their lives become a long tunnel with no exit, where dieting is an end in itself, not a way to lose a few pounds.

What Are Eating Rituals?

People with anorexia and other eating disorders often do odd things with their food or have strange rules they follow before they can eat. These behaviors help them feel less anxious about eating or about life in general. People also use food rituals to make it look like they are eating more than they are. Typical behaviors include:

- Cutting food into very small pieces so it takes longer to eat
- Being unable to eat or prepare food in front of other people
- Keeping foods from touching each other on the plate
- Chewing food a certain number of times
- Eating foods in a special order
- Pushing food around the plate so it looks like it is being eaten

In anorexia, people commonly deny themselves food because what they eat and how much they weigh are things they have power over when the rest of their life seems out of control.

People with anorexia hide their disorder or avoid social activities that involve eating, often withdrawing from family and friends. This isolation causes them to feel alone and depressed; it works the opposite way, too, because people who already feel alone and depressed are more likely to develop anorexia.

HOW REAL PEOPLE DEAL: BAILEY'S EATING RITUALS

When Bailey was in ninth grade, she transferred to a new, very competitive high school. The classes were hard and she did not have any friends at first, which left her feeling overwhelmed and alone.

That year, she started developing food rituals. For example, she would cut her food into small pieces and eat with her hands instead of using utensils. For some reason, this made her feel less stressed out.

The rituals got worse. By the time Bailey was fifteen she had so many rules about food she could hardly eat. For instance, she allowed herself diet frozen dinners, but not carrots. And every night, she ate an ice cream sandwich while she watched her favorite TV show. But that was the only time she allowed herself anything fattening.

Deep down, Bailey knew these rules did not make sense, but she felt powerless to stop making them. Breaking the rules made her feel disgusted with herself, but not eating and throwing food away made her feel guilty, too. In the end, it was easier just to skip meals. Her parents were very worried and so were her friends. When they told her she looked skinny and suggested that she had an eating disorder, she denied it. But hearing she looked too thin actually made her feel good.

On Bailey's fifteenth birthday, she told herself that she could eat just one piece of birthday cake; otherwise, she could not go to the mall later on. But then she kept picking at the cake, wanting another slice and hating herself.

At the mall, while her friends ate burgers, Bailey sat with a plate of fries, making them last by dipping them over and over in ketchup. At home that night, she went online and filled out a survey called, "Do You Have an Eating

Disorder?" Her score told her she needed help, but she was still in denial.

A few weeks later, Bailey's parents got so worried, they took her to a therapist. Bailey was admitted to a residential treatment center for eating disorders and diagnosed with anorexia. After eight weeks, she was well enough to go home. Today, she is able to enjoy food again. But she will never forget her ordeal.

"When you have food rituals, your mind tells you that doing them is going to keep you from gaining weight, keep you accepted, keep you comfortable, keep you from failing," Bailey said. "But no food behavior can do any of those things. It's just going to make you feel worse."[7]

Cutting food into small pieces is one food ritual.

Sometimes people with anorexia will cook for others because they cannot get their minds off food.

Not all people with anorexia continue to starve themselves. Up to half eventually alternate restricting food with binge eating and then try to counteract this by purging—getting rid of the food or calories in various ways (such as vomiting, taking laxatives, or exercising excessively). This type of anorexia is called binge-eating/purging type. The other type of anorexia, called restricting type, does not involve bingeing or purging. These are the only two officially recognized types. But experts agree that other variations of anorexia exist and many eating disorders overlap.

BULIMIA NERVOSA

People suffering from bulimia nervosa associate their body shape and weight with their self-worth and feel out of control while eating. This disorder has many things in common with anorexia, but there is one key difference: People with bulimia *often* binge eat, although they may alternate these episodes with periods of dieting or fasting (going without food).

Binge eating involves consuming huge amounts of food rapidly at one sitting. Binges can range from 1,000 calories (about half of a normal day's food intake for an active young adult woman) to about 30,000 calories (15 days' worth of food).[8, 9] Some people have been known to eat as many as 50,000 calories in a few hours![10]

Binges are done in private, and people may hide food to binge on when they are alone. They barely taste the food, wolfing down whole pizzas, fast-food meals, entire cakes or bags of chips, and two-liter bottles of soda. They stop eating when stomach pain becomes unbearable, when they fall asleep (often with food still in their hands or mouths),

Gut Reactions

Stomach and intestinal problems are common in people with anorexia and purging-type bulimia. Most of these problems go away when people start eating or stop vomiting and abusing diuretics and laxatives. But some problems are permanent or life-threatening.

When people eat very little, food takes a long time to travel from the stomach through the digestive tract, because the intestines stop working efficiently. This slow transit time causes gas, a full feeling, stomach pain, and constipation. Laxative abuse also causes constipation.

After vomiting, taking diuretics, or taking laxatives, water and electrolytes are lost. Electrolytes are salts and minerals that are critically important to the body, regulating fluid balance and helping with muscle contraction and energy generation. Severe dehydration (excessive water loss) and electrolyte imbalance can cause seizures, permanent kidney problems, and irregular heartbeats. What's more, the stomach acid in vomit can seriously damage the esophagus. In extreme cases, forceful vomiting can blow a hole in the wall of the esophagus. This medical emergency, known as Boerhaave's syndrome, can lead to infection and death unless the patient has surgery immediately.

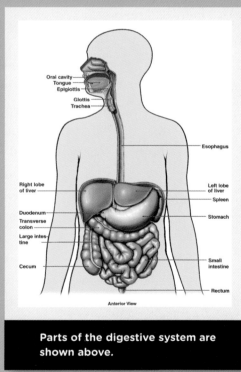

Parts of the digestive system are shown above.

or when someone interrupts them. To officially be diagnosed with bulimia, people must binge at least twice a week for three months.

People with "purging type" bulimia counteract the binge as soon as possible with forced vomiting, taking laxatives or diuretics, or giving themselves enemas. In severe cases, people purge several times a day or after eating only small amounts of food. People with "non-purging type" bulimia use other types of behaviors to cancel out eating, such as excessive exercise or fasting.

How many Americans have bulimia? No one knows for sure because many people never go for treatment. Also, statistics for eating disorders are usually lumped together, with 10 million women and 1 million men being the number most often reported.[11] We do know that bulimia cases are increasing and that it is more common than anorexia. In some studies, 2 to 7 percent of the people surveyed had bulimia.[12]

Eighty percent of people with bulimia are female, and 1 to 2 percent of teens and young adult women are thought to be affected.[13] Bulimia also occurs in boys and men, especially those in sports or occupations that have a weight requirement, such as wrestling or being a jockey.

Unlike anorexia, people with bulimia are not easy to recognize because they are often of normal weight. However, some are slightly underweight or even obese. Many people with bulimia go to work or school, get married, and lead outwardly normal lives. They keep their bulimia a secret for years, even from their husbands or wives. Others with bulimia binge and purge so

While 80 percent of people with bulimia are female, males suffer from the binge-purge cycle, too.

often, they have no time for a normal life or close relationships. Bingeing and purging *is* their life.

Doctors may also have trouble identifying patients with bulimia because they often look healthy. But because frequent vomiting can damage the teeth and gums, dentists are often the first to recognize a case of bulimia.

To officially be diagnosed with bulimia, people must binge at least twice a week for three months.

What are the other outward signs? Suspect bulimia if a friend or family member often visits the bathroom right after eating; smells of vomit; has calluses on the back of her hands and knuckles (from sticking her hands down her throat to force vomiting); or has facial swelling or "chipmunk face" (from salivary gland enlargement caused by vomiting). Other signs include avoiding friends or not taking part in usual activities, exercising excessively, and constantly talking about dieting. People who live with a binge eater may notice that large amounts of food keep disappearing and find empty food packages or candy wrappers in the trash.

No one knows how many people die from complications of bulimia, but it is not thought to be as deadly as anorexia. Even so, bulimia causes complications that can range from relatively minor to life-threatening. For example, people who vomit may have a constant sore throat or heartburn (pain in the chest due to irritation from stomach acid). Those who abuse laxatives may have constipation. Serious complications include severe dehydration (loss of body water), kidney problems from diuretic use, and ruptured esophagus from vomiting.

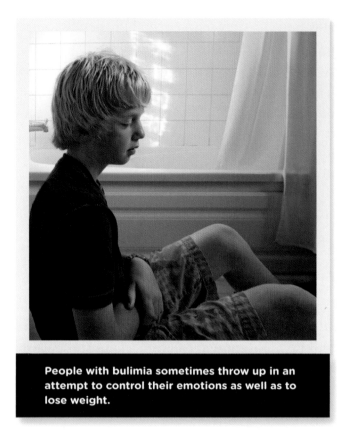

People with bulimia sometimes throw up in an attempt to control their emotions as well as to lose weight.

Vomiting can also cause imbalances in chemicals and other substances in the body. These imbalances can result in irregular heartbeats and heart failure, kidney failure, and other deadly complications.

People with bulimia have trouble controlling their moods as well as their eating. Besides getting rid of food, purging is a method they use to calm them, release angry feelings, and cope with emotions or problems they cannot handle. When describing why they binge and purge, people with bulimia often say things like, "Something comes over me and I can't help myself," or "I feel that there is a monster inside of me."[14] Unlike people with anorexia, who are in tight control of their eating, people suffering from bulimia feel completely out of control. But they also feel depressed, isolated, and ashamed, just like people with anorexia.

Dental Health and Eating Disorders

People with bulimia often see a dentist before a doctor. Why? Because frequent vomiting can cause severe tooth pain and other dental problems. Vomiting exposes the teeth to stomach acid, which can destroy the inner layer of teeth, leaving only a thin, semi-transparent outer layer of enamel. Teeth may also become short, brittle, weak, decayed, and highly sensitive to hot and cold food. Dry mouth, cracked lips, and exposed gums (known as gingival recession) can lead to tooth loss, and enlarged salivary glands may also develop. These problems develop in up to 89 percent of people with bulimia.[15]

BINGE-EATING DISORDER

Binge-eating disorder, which used to be called compulsive overeating, is similar to bulimia. However, people with this disorder do not purge after they eat. That is part of the reason why many of them are overweight or obese. Binge-eating disorder is officially listed under the heading of eating disorders not otherwise specified. However, so many people have it that most experts consider it a separate eating disorder.

Those with binge-eating disorder can have food binges that last for a whole day, not just a few hours like in bulimia. But the bingeing itself and the reasons for doing it are similar to bulimia. People eat very fast until their stomachs are stretched and painful. They eat alone because they are embarrassed and ashamed of their behavior. And they say they cannot control themselves. Often, bingeing is how they calm themselves and handle things that cause stress in their lives.

Those with binge-eating disorder can have food binges that last for a whole day, not just a few hours like in bulimia.

Some experts believe there are two types of binge eating. The first type, deprivation-sensitive binge eating, usually occurs after someone goes on a diet or deprives himself of food. Bingeing is an extreme reaction to this. The second type, addictive or dissociative binge eating, arises from a need to soothe oneself through food. People escape through bingeing, saying it makes them feel calm, numb, and detached.

Only about one-fourth of obese people are binge eaters.[16] Some obese people eat a lot of fattening foods or nibble all day long, but they do not binge. Binge-eating disorder is a psychological problem; obesity is a physical one.

Binge-eating disorder is thought to occur in 1 to 5 percent of the U.S. population. About 60 percent of sufferers are women, and 40 percent are men.[17] This disorder can cause grave, even deadly, health problems related to obesity, including diabetes, heart disease, and high blood pressure.

For many, binge eating is brought on by stress.

EATING DISORDERS NOT OTHERWISE SPECIFIED (EDNOS)

Eating disorders that do not fit under the strict categories of anorexia or bulimia are called eating disorders not otherwise specified (EDNOS). These disorders are very similar to anorexia and bulimia, except one or two key features are missing or different. For example, a woman may have all the anorexia symptoms but still get menstrual periods, or she may weigh slightly too much to be considered anorexic. Or she might binge only twice a month instead of twice a week.

An estimated one-third of all people treated by doctors for eating disorders are in the EDNOS category.[18] Unfortunately, many do not get the treatment they need because their insurance companies will not pay for diseases whose symptoms vary even slightly from the descriptions of anorexia or bulimia found in the official manual called the *DSM-IV-TR* (see "What Is the *DSM-IV-TR*?" on page 40).

OTHER EATING DISORDERS

Although they are not listed as eating disorders in the *DSM-IV-TR*, the following disorders involve bizarre and often very harmful behaviors.

Night-eating syndrome: Skipping breakfast and then eating more and more as the day goes on is typical of this syndrome. People with this disorder eat dinner, and then continue eating, consuming more than half of their daily food after dinner. In this respect, they resemble people with binge-eating disorder.

People with night-eating syndrome have insomnia, the inability to fall asleep or stay asleep. They wake up one or more times during the night and eat, which makes them feel guilty, ashamed, and depressed. Because they do not get a good night's sleep, they also suffer from daytime sleepiness, which can make concentrating difficult and driving dangerous.

What Is the *DSM-IV-TR*?

The letters above are an abbreviation for *Diagnostic and Statistical Manual for Mental Disorders, Volume 4, Text Revision*. This manual describes all the mental illnesses officially recognized by the American Psychiatric Association and gives each a code number. Anorexia nervosa, bulimia nervosa, and eating disorders not otherwise specified (EDNOS) are listed as separate categories. Binge-eating disorder is included as a type of EDNOS.

Doctors use the information in the manual to diagnose (identify) a patient's eating disorder. Then they enter the code number into the patient's medical records and send the information to the patient's insurance company. The insurance company then pays at least part of the cost of the treatment.

Problems occur when patients do not quite fit the mold. For example, if a woman has all the symptoms of anorexia but is not quite thin enough, she does not fit the official definition of anorexia according to the *DSM-IV*. Therefore, insurance companies will not pay for her treatment.

Some experts feel the *DSM-IV* definitions are too rigid and that they actually encourage people to get sicker so they will be able to get insurance coverage. The last time the *DSM-IV* was revised was 1994. Another revision is scheduled for 2011. Perhaps some needed changes will occur then.[19]

Surveys reveal that about 1.5 percent of adults in the general population have night-eating syndrome, but as many as 27 percent of severely obese adults have it.[20] More than half of patients trace the start of the disorder to a very stressful life event.

Sleep-eating disorder: People with this disorder eat while they are asleep. They sleepwalk into the kitchen and prepare

Purging Prevents Weight Gain

Purging does not prevent weight gain as much as people think. By the time a binge is over and vomiting begins, most food has already left the stomach, entered the small intestine, and been absorbed into the bloodstream. After vomiting, the body holds onto about 1,200 calories of the binge food.[21]

Purging with laxatives after eating does not cause weight loss, either. Food is absorbed in the small intestine, but laxatives only affect the large intestine. Because laxatives cause watery diarrhea, people imagine they are losing all the calories they just ate. After laxative use, only 12 percent fewer calories are absorbed.[22]

The third method of purging, taking diuretics (pills that cause excessive urination and water loss), may cause a drop in weight from the water lost in urine, but this is only temporary.

Purging does not necessarily prevent weight gain.

food, although they do not always binge eat. They may have a vague sense of what is happening or may wake up in the morning with food or candy wrappers in their beds and no recollection of what happened.

At least 65 percent of people with sleep-eating disorder eat buttered cigarettes, frozen food, and other inedible substances that can hurt them. (A compulsion to eat nonfood items while conscious is known as pica, which can sometimes stem from nutritional deficiencies or developmental problems.) An estimated 5 percent of the general population has this disorder and up to 17 percent of people who have other eating disorders have it. More than 40 percent of sufferers are overweight, and more than 65 percent are female.[23]

Purging disorder: Behaviors of people suffering from this disorder include vomiting, taking laxatives, or performing other purging behaviors without bingeing.

Body dysmorphic disorder: This is not an eating disorder, but it may occur along with one. Sufferers of this disorder have distorted body images—they do not see themselves as they really are. If they are obsessed with weight and convinced they are fat when they are not, they may also have anorexia or bulimia.

Body dysmorphic disorder may be about weight or muscles, but it can also be about other body parts the person is not happy with. Some sufferers believe their skin, nose, hair, or other features are so ugly, they rarely leave the house. They look in mirrors constantly, try to cover up their "defects," and even consult with plastic surgeons. The disorder usually starts in the teen or early adult years and affects males and females equally.

Although these less common disorders are still being studied, those suffering from these problems can improve with medicine, counseling, and family support.

CHAPTER THREE

History of Eating Disorders

Karen Carpenter and her brother Richard were one of the most popular music duos of the 1970s. The sister and brother act, known as the Carpenters, had a string of number one hits, recorded eight gold and five platinum albums, made five television specials, and toured all over the world. Their soft rock sound appealed to music lovers everywhere and won them three Grammy awards. But in 1983, Karen Carpenter died unexpectedly from heart failure. She was only thirty-two years old. Heart disease usually occurs in people much older, so why did it take the life of someone so young?

Although Karen was a popular singer and musician, she had always been insecure about her looks. Her brother recalled that she was "a little overweight" as a teenager and went on a diet when she was seventeen. Karen lost twenty to twenty-five pounds and kept them off for several years.[1] But she never lost her insecurity about her appearance. In 1973, she began to diet again and this time it took a dangerous turn. By 1975, she weighed only ninety-one pounds and had to take time off from performing to recover. It was downhill from there.

Karen continued to lose weight. She took large doses of thyroid medication (although her thyroid was normal) and used massive amounts of laxatives each day. By the time she realized how sick she was, she weighed only eighty pounds. She went to a therapist for help, but it was too late. The autopsy following her death showed that she had been abusing ipecac—a dangerous substance that causes vomiting and can damage the heart muscle, especially if used more than once.

Karen Carpenter accepts an award from Emmylou Harris at the Billboard Music Awards in January 1977. Carpenter's death from anorexia brought awareness of the disease to a new level in America.

(When health professionals learn that a patient has taken ipecac, they usually advise him to head straight to a hospital emergency room!) Karen had been suffering from an eating disorder, anorexia nervosa, which then caused the heart failure that killed her.

Until the 1970s, most people had never heard of anorexia nervosa. Psychologists and behavioral scientists knew about it, of course, and the media had begun to write about the disease. But nobody took it seriously. Karen Carpenter's death brought attention to the disorder and made the public aware of just how dangerous eating disorders could be.

fact OR fiction

People Vomited in Places Called Vomitoria in Ancient Rome

Vomitoria (the plural of vomitorium) really existed in Rome, but not for vomiting. A vomitorium was a passageway into a Roman amphitheater, a round or oval structure with tiers of seats that rose gradually from an open space in the center. Spectators could quickly get to their seats through the vomitorium and, just as quickly, exit at the end of a performance. Since the word *vomitorium* comes from Latin, meaning "to vomit, vomit forth, or throw up," perhaps the purpose of a vomitorium was to "vomit" people from the amphitheater. It is true that Roman nobles enjoyed their feasts so much they often vomited to make room for the next delicacy. They just didn't have a special room for it.[2]

Vomitoria were a common feature of ancient Roman architecture but they weren't used for vomiting.

St. Jerome, pictured above, was a major figure in Christianity in the fourth century. His teachings led some of his female followers to deny themselves food, and one of them died of starvation in 383 A.D., becoming the first recorded death from anorexia.

EARLY HISTORY

Anorexia, bulimia, and binge eating might be thought of as modern diseases, but research suggests that our ancient ancestors suffered from eating disorders as well. Written references from ancient times describe behaviors that are similar. For instance, reports from classical Greece (c. 500–323 B.C.) describe people overeating. Later accounts (c. 323–146 B.C.) tell of male hermits starving themselves as a way of renouncing the material world. The Greek historian Herodotus (c. 484–430 B.C.) traveled to Egypt where he observed people purging for three days every month for health reasons. And, in the first century A.D., the philosopher Seneca wrote this about his fellow Romans: "They eat to vomit and vomit to eat."[3]

During the early Christian era in Europe, the doctrine of Gnosticism was popular. It had its roots in Eastern religion and promoted the belief that the body is evil and the spirit or soul is holy. Many well-to-do Roman women adopted these ideas and were known to starve themselves. One woman, a member of a group led by Saint Jerome, died from starvation in 383 A.D. Hers was the first anorexia death to be recorded.

THE INFLUENCE OF SOCIETY

Self-imposed starvation seemed to go out of style during the Dark Ages in Europe (c. 476–1200 A.D.). Only three cases of anorexia were recorded. Why? Researchers believe it's because economic and social factors make a difference when it comes to eating disorders. Since the Dark Ages was a time of wars, famines, and plagues, women had to be physically strong and able to have children. Eating well was essential for survival.[4]

The late Middle Ages and the Renaissance period that followed was another story. As wealth returned to the cities of southern Europe, anorexia became popular again, especially for religious reasons. In the book *Holy Anorexia* Rudolph Bell writes about 181 anorexic women between 1200 and 1600 A.D. who starved themselves to get closer to God. Being thin became a sign of religious devotion and these women were seen as channels to God. Most of the women, who came from somewhat affluent families, joined religious orders. The Roman Catholic Church honored some of these women with sainthood, such as Catherine of Siena (1347–1380), who was influ-ential with the leaders of her time. Catherine was known to make herself vomit by pushing a stick down her throat after she ate.

Saint Catherine of Siena (1347–1380) was known to make herself vomit, a behavior associated with the disease now called bulimia.

As wealth returned to the cities of southern Europe, anorexia became popular again, especially for religious reasons.

Some researchers argue that, psychologically speaking, starving yourself for religious reasons is not the same as starving yourself to be more attractive. Others disagree. Key factors in eating disorders include the need for control or power. These researchers believe that control was an issue for women like Catherine, who lived in a society run by men. Women had little or no say in family decisions and were subject to arranged marriages. Maybe Catherine's insistence on refusing food and entering a convent was the only way she could control her life and world. Also, her suffering gave her a place of respect and power in the community that was not usually available to women of her time. After her death from starvation at age thirty-three, dozens of young girls tried to follow in her footsteps by starving themselves, too.[5]

Who Were the "Fasting Girls?"

In the seventeenth century, fasting girls or "miraculous maids" were young girls who claimed to be able to live for long periods of time without food. They usually came from poor families who lived in rural areas. Many starved themselves for religious reasons. Some became famous, some were considered fakes, and some died of malnutrition.

The earliest recorded mention of a fasting girl was in 1613. Jane Balan was an eleven-year-old French girl who allegedly went without food or drink for three years. According to the report, her stomach grew thin and she stopped passing urine and bowel movements. However, her arms, breasts, and hair supposedly looked normal and she continued to menstruate. She was also normally active, working around the house and going to the market for food.

In 1669, an English girl named Martha Taylor claimed she had lived with almost no food or drink for thirteen months. A group of physicians, who watched her closely for more than two weeks, were unable to detect any fraud.

Stories of fasting girls continued throughout the Victorian period. In 1813, an Englishwoman named Ann Moore claimed she had eaten no solid food (except for a few currants one day in June) since 1807 and had drunk nothing since 1808. When she was placed under close watch, her condition deteriorated. It improved after the watch was called off. In the end, she confessed to eating during her six-year fast.

Sarah Jacob was known as the "Welsh Fasting Girl." After an illness at age thirteen, she had a problem with eating. From October 1867 to December 1869, she and her family insisted she had not eaten. She became known as a "miraculous faster," and people came from all over the area to visit her. What they found was a bedridden young girl, dressed as a bride with a flowered wreath on her head. Many were moved to leave money. When a group of medical professionals placed her under close watch, however, her condition worsened. Her parents refused to intervene for fear of killing her, and she died after eighteen days. It is likely that Sarah was secretly eating during her fast, although her parents may not have been aware of it.[6]

During the Reformation and rise of Protestantism, the Catholic Church insisted that people could commune with God only through priests—who were all male. Also, the role of women in society changed again. Their ability to bear children became more important than their appearance, and self-starvation declined.

During the Victorian Era (1831–1901), there was a surge of anorexia cases, especially among upper- and middle-class girls. The Industrial Revolution created a new, sophisticated middle class with money and culture. Being a thin woman became a sign of wealth and status in society. Also, food was a symbol of sexuality to Victorian women. So if a young girl wanted to be seen as pure, avoiding food was one way to do it.

EARLY MEDICAL LITERATURE

The earliest medical account of anorexia, *A Treatise of Consumption*, was published in 1689 by Dr. Richard Morton in London. In it, he referred to the disorder as "nervous consumption," due to "sadness and anxious cares." He described how the disease caused the bodies of his two patients—a young woman and a sixteen-year-old boy—to waste away. At first, Morton treated them with the medicine available at the time. When this failed and the young woman died, he tried something different. He suggested the boy leave his chaotic home life and move to the country. No one knows if the second treatment worked.[7]

Queen Victoria's surgeon William Gull coined the term *anorexia nervosa*.

It was not until 175 years later, in 1862, that French physician Louis Victor Marcé wrote that anorexia was not a physical ailment, but a psychiatric one. He recommended removing patients from their homes, where vivid emotions might interfere with treatment, and placing them with strangers. Marcé also suggested force feeding, if necessary, and warned about the possibility of relapse and the need for long-term care.[8]

In 1873, Charles Lesègue, professor of clinical medicine in the Faculty of Medicine of Paris, described the medical symptoms of anorexia nervosa in his report *On Hysterical Anorexia*. He saw it as a psychological disorder but did not recommend any treatment or medication. Instead, he advised doctors to take a watchful approach. As a patient gradually developed the side effects of the disease, according to Lesègue, her relatives would become upset. Their "sad appearance" would, in turn, cause the patient to become anxious herself. That was the moment, said Lesègue, when the doctor should step in.[9]

A month after Lesègue's report, Dr. William Gull, a physician to Queen Victoria, presented his own brief report, titled *Anorexia Nervosa*. The disease now had a name. Gull also believed it was a psychological disorder, but his recommendations differed from those of Lesègue. Gull believed that letting the starvation process continue was dangerous. Warmth, rest, and a steady food supply would help the patient regain her strength and recover.[10]

UNDERSTANDING ANOREXIA NERVOSA

For the first few decades of the early twentieth century, other physicians expressed their viewpoints about the nature of anorexia nervosa, ranging from a hormone deficiency to tuberculosis. By the late 1930s, however, researchers realized that eating disorders involved emotional and psychological problems, not just physical ones.

Although the disease was not common during the two world wars, the late 1960s saw a surge in cases. In 1973, Hilde Bruch argued in her book, *Eating Disorders*, that self-starvation was really a struggle for control and self-respect. According to Bruch, patients with anorexia nervosa had three problems: They had a distorted concept of body image, were unable to recognize the need for nutrition, and felt ineffective.[11] Bruch believed that psychotherapy would help a patient find his or her "genuine self" by challenging wrong beliefs and nurturing true feelings.[12]

The American Psychiatric Association officially classified anorexia nervosa as a mental disorder in 1980.

In 1973, Hilde Bruch argued in her book, *Eating Disorders*, that self-starvation was really a struggle for control and self-respect.

BULIMIA—A NEW EATING DISORDER?

In the late nineteenth century, physicians began to notice the symptoms of bulimia, mostly in the form of binge eating among anorexia patients. For a while, some physicians believed bulimia was a symptom of anorexia. A few women with bulimia were also noted during the early twentieth century. Ellen West (a pseudonym) was one. In 1944, her psychiatrist, Ludwig Binswanger, used excerpts from her diary to write about her life. (See "How Real People Deal" on page 52.)

HOW REAL PEOPLE DEAL: THE CASE OF ELLEN WEST*

Ellen lived in West Switzerland during the turn of the twentieth century. She was a bright young girl, read a lot, and wrote poetry. As a teenager, she wanted to be the best at everything.

When she was twenty, Ellen went on vacation to Sicily. She enjoyed the food so much that she gained a little weight. Unfortunately, some of her girlfriends teased her about it. Ellen was so upset she began to fast and go on long hikes for exercise. She may have lost weight, but she gained a fear of getting fat. It depressed her.

Ellen became interested in social work. She disliked the upper class society from which she came, but felt powerless to change it. She wrote in her diary that she felt tied down by "the chains of conventionality." Ellen had doubts about the purpose of her life. She had a family history of depression and suicide on both sides. Even at a young age, she had a fascination for how short life was and how useless it seemed. At seventeen she had written a poem about death that made it sound strangely appealing.

At twenty-one Ellen entered college, but had a breakdown and left. By the time she was twenty-three, she was not just afraid of being fat, she also had an intense craving for food, particularly sweets.

At twenty-four, Ellen fell into a serious depression. She began to believe that being thin was the key to her happiness. She took long walks to lose weight and swallowed large numbers of thyroid pills every day. When her doctor prescribed bed rest, it caused her to regain weight. Depressed, she fought hard to lose it again.

A few years later, Ellen got married, hoping it would help get rid of her obsession. A year later, she had a miscarriage.

* Not her real name

Having a baby would have meant eating the healthy food she desperately wanted to avoid.

Ellen's illness grew more serious. She became a vegetarian and took sixty or seventy laxative tablets a day. She vomited every night and had diarrhea during the day. Her weight dropped to ninety-two pounds and her obsession with food worsened. She missed meals, but ate several pounds of tomatoes and twenty oranges each day.

Ellen was admitted to a sanatorium. Two different psychiatrists had been unable to help her. She had made two suicide attempts. Sanatorium employees described her as devouring food like a wild animal, but she still lost weight. Ellen wanted to die. She wrote:

> Everything agitates me, and I experience every agitation and a sensation of hunger, even if I have just eaten.
> I am afraid of myself. I am afraid of the feelings to which I am defenselessly delivered over every minute.
> I am in prison and cannot get out.[13]

Ellen's doctor knew about her suicide threats, but thought there was nothing he could do for her. Three days after the doctor discharged her, Ellen enjoyed a meal with her husband, eating freely for the first time in thirteen years. She ate some chocolates, went for a walk with her husband, read some poetry, and wrote a few letters. She then took a lethal dose of poison. The next morning she was dead. She was only thirty-three.

Twenty years later, Ellen's doctor, Ludwig Binswanger, wrote about her story in a case history called "The Case of Ellen West." He believed she was schizophrenic and that there was no cure. He does not mention her eating problem,

Continued on next page

Continued from previous page

although eating disorders such as anorexia were known by the medical world at the time.

Ellen's story is a sad one. She probably had bulimia. If Ellen had lived in our time, modern medicine may have been able to help her.

A Poem by Ellen West
I'd like to die just as the birdling does
That splits his throat in highest jubilation;
And not to live as the worm on earth lives on,
Becoming old and ugly, dull and dumb!
No, feel for once how forces in me kindle,
And wildly be consumed in my own fire.[14]

SAY
what

What Do *Anorexia Nervosa* and *Bulimia Nervosa* Mean?

The word *anorexia* comes from Greek. *An* means "without" and *orexis* means "appetite." Put them together and it means "without appetite." Some dictionaries call it "loss of appetite," which can occur with many diseases. The term *anorexia nervosa* refers specifically to the psychological disorder.

The word *bulimia* also comes from Greek. *Bous* means "ox" in Greek and *limos* is "hunger." Strictly speaking, bulimia is "ox-hunger." Most people have probably heard the expression "as hungry as an ox." It is a good way to describe how people with bulimia often feel when they are bingeing.

Nervosa comes from Latin for "nervous." Anorexia nervosa literally means "loss of appetite for nervous reasons," and bulimia nervosa is, of course, "ox-hunger for nervous reasons."

By the 1970s, bulimia was becoming more known as a disorder. British psychiatrist Gerald Russell named it "bulimia nervosa" in 1979, describing it as a variation of anorexia nervosa. According to Russell, patients with bulimia nervosa had to meet three criteria: the urge to overeat, a fear of being fat, and the use of laxatives and/or vomiting to avoid getting fat.

Bulimia nervosa was classified as a mental disorder in 1987 by the American Psychiatric Association.

BINGE-EATING DISORDER—THE LATEST THREAT

While bulimia nervosa is a relatively new disorder, binge eating has been around for centuries. Ironically, the term "binge-eating disorder" was only introduced in 1992. It describes people who go on eating binges but do not fast or purge to lose weight. Binge eating is often associated with obesity, although people who are obese are not necessarily binge eaters. Binge-eating disorder has not yet been classified as a mental disorder in the *DSM-IV-TR*, but many health care professionals think it should be. It is rapidly becoming the most common eating disorder in this country, yet it is still considered an EDNOS.

Most of the early historical information on eating disorders was discovered in the second half of the twentieth century, thanks to the hard work of modern researchers. Learning why these diseases flourish or decline in different societies helps physicians treat them.

EATING DISORDERS TODAY

For decades, researchers have studied eating disorders in young women who were white and middle or upper class. These women usually lived in Western cultures, such as Canada, Britain, Europe, Australia, and especially the United States, where being thin was—and still is—the ideal. By the end of the twentieth century, however, cases of eating disorders had

Eating disorders affect both genders and all economic, ethnic, and cultural backgrounds.

appeared in other countries as well. They were also showing up in men, as well as in different age groups and races.

Women in non-Western countries, who had previously seemed more comfortable with their bodies than women in Western cultures, were developing body image issues, too. Many researchers believe it is due to the spread of Western culture, which has extended its influence to at least forty different countries, including China, India, Mexico, and South Africa.[15] The greater the exposure to Western ideals of thinness, the more likely women in these countries were to develop eating disorders.

In the United States, eating disorders were showing up among ethnic groups, too. The popular opinion was that non-Caucasian women were immune to diseases like anorexia, because their cultures were more accepting of different body sizes. But risk factors for eating disorders and disordered eating patterns were becoming more common among African-American, Latina, Asian-American, and Native American teens.

It is now believed that people from all economic, ethnic, and cultural backgrounds, as well as both genders, are at risk for eating disorders.

A 1996 study reported that young Latina and Asian-American girls were unhappier about their bodies than white girls.[16] Another study among Native American teens in 1997 found that 48 percent of girls and 30 percent of boys in grades seven through twelve had dieted in the previous year. Also, 28 percent of girls and 21 percent of boys had purged.[17] Eating disorders were also more common among African-American women than people first thought, especially when it came to binge eating and using laxatives.[18]

Men and boys also entered the picture, as well as low-income people and middle-aged women. But most alarming was the number of young children who were showing risk factors for eating disorders. In a 1997 study of eight- to ten-year-olds, 10 to 20 percent of boys and 13 to 41 percent of girls had already tried to lose weight through dieting, diet foods, or exercise.[19] A 1991 Australian study found that 42 percent of girls in the first, second, and third grades wanted to be thinner.[20]

It is now believed that people from all economic, ethnic, and cultural backgrounds, as well as both genders, are at risk for eating disorders. But little research has been done on these groups. Although many scientists agree that Western culture has played a significant part in spreading the diseases, others believe it is more complex than that.

Is bulimia different for a boy than for a girl? How does poverty affect self-esteem? Can an eating disorder be a response to the stress of racism? Studying different groups helps researchers understand how eating disorders affect people from all backgrounds.

CHAPTER FOUR

Risk Factors and Preventing Eating Disorders

A re eating disorders on the rise? What causes them? Why are some people more likely to get eating disorders than others? And is there any way to prevent them? Health experts are asking the same questions, and the answers are often as complicated as the conditions. But one thing is certain: If people want to learn how to prevent disease, they need to understand why it occurs in the first place.

ARE EATING DISORDERS ON THE RISE?

Most experts agree that the incidence of eating disorders has increased over the past thirty or forty years. In 2007, the United States population was about 300 million. A national survey published that year found that 1.3 million women and 450,000 men had anorexia at some point in their lives. The numbers for bulimia were 2.25 million women and 775,000 men.

The most common eating disorder, binge eating, had been experienced by 5.25 million women and 3 million men.[1] That statistic is not surprising, considering the significant obesity problem in the United States today. The survey also found that lifetime rates of eating disorders were higher among younger groups, suggesting that the disorders are becoming more common.[2]

The lead author of the study, Dr. James I. Hudson, said the study had one major limitation. It was based on self-reports. Since people tend to underreport eating disorder problems, the actual statistics are probably higher.[3]

Are Eating Disorders Different in Men?

The answer is yes and no. Men and boys have eating disorders for the same reasons as women and girls. Their symptoms are the same, too. But there are a few differences.

Men with eating disorders often diet because they were teased for being overweight as children. They also lose weight to prevent medical illnesses, especially ones that other family members have.

Athletic men who lose weight to improve on their performance have an even greater chance of developing an eating disorder. To get to their goal, however, they are less likely than women to vomit or abuse laxatives and more likely to exercise compulsively.[4]

Eating disorders can sometimes affect men, particularly male athletes, in different ways than women.

Getting treatment is more difficult for men. They tend to see eating disorders as a "woman's disease" and are less likely to ask for help. Meanwhile, eating disorders in men are only starting to get attention, and few services are designed for them. When a man with an eating disorder *does* look for help, he may find himself the only man in a group of women. An effort needs to be made to raise awareness of eating disorders in men and work to prevent them.

WHAT CAUSES EATING DISORDERS?

Many people think that an eating disorder is just an obsession with food and weight, but the disorder is a lot more complex. According to the Office on Women's Health for the U.S. Department of Health and Human Services, there is no single cause. Culture, families, psychological or personality traits, life changes or stressful events, and biology all contribute to a person's eating disorder.[5] To make it more complicated, these factors interact in many different ways.

Cultural Influence

Each society has its own set of beliefs and attitudes that shape the behavior of its members. For decades now, Western culture has held up thinness as an ideal, especially among women. In America, many people mistakenly believe that they cannot be beautiful, happy, or successful, unless they are thin. Americans—who are also competitive and like to succeed—are completely hooked on this thinness ideal.[6]

The Media: The media, of course, do their best to get the message across that thin is beautiful. Magazines, movies, music videos, the Internet, and television shows bombard the public with glamorous images of girls and women who look slender and fragile. Teenage girls, whose bodies are still developing, are especially vulnerable to these images. Like everyone else, they want to be special. Unfortunately, some buy into the media's message that being special means being thin. When these teens compare themselves to their favorite stars—some of whom look emaciated—they often end up disappointed. A 2002 study showed that girls who identify with television stars, read teen magazines, and watch television programs that idealize a thin body are more likely to be unhappy with their own bodies.[7]

Advertising is one of the worst offenders at keeping the thin ideal alive. The average American is exposed to a whopping 5,000 advertising messages a day.[8] Magazines are filled with pictures of supermodels who look much thinner than their counterparts did a few decades ago. Today's average female model weighs up to 23 percent less than today's average woman. Many of the photos are airbrushed

On TV, it might seem that everyone is extremely thin and beautiful.

or computer enhanced. So girls are not just comparing themselves to images that are unrealistic. They are not even *real*.[9]

Television commercials are just as misleading. Female models and their bodies sell everything from cars to food (another irony). In one study, girls who viewed commercials showing thin models felt less confident about their bodies and were more worried about their weight and appearance.[10] But advertising firms have no plans to change their tactics. Not as long as women and girls are more likely to buy the brand a thin model is selling.[11]

A 1995 study in Fiji showed just how influential television can be. Dr. Anne Becker studied TV's impact on adolescent girls in this 2,000-year-old culture, which had always promoted a healthy appetite and body size. Before television, the girls had never dieted or had eating disorders. A month after it was introduced, they began dieting for the first time. Three years later, Becker found that 11 percent of the girls had started vomiting to lose weight.[12]

Dieting: The pressure is on for American women and girls to achieve the "perfect body." It might explain why the diet industry is such a huge business. Americans spend over 40 billion dollars a year on dieting and diet products.[13] Every month or so, a new diet hits the market, promising to "really work." The truth is that most diets only work for a while. One study showed that 95 percent of dieters regain their lost weight in one to five years.[14] Dieting is a serious risk factor for eating disorders. In fact, girls who diet have a seven to eight times *greater* chance of getting an eating disorder than girls who do not.[15] One reason diets work so poorly may be the set-point theory. This theory argues that each person has his or her own control system for body fat. Some set points are high and some are low. Also, people cannot control their set point, which varies from person to person. According to this theory, when a person diets and quickly goes below her set point, her body thinks she is starving and reacts by slowing down her metabolism. It will do whatever it can to get her back to her natural set point,

What Is a Food Pyramid for Healthy Eating?

Healthy eating is one of the best ways to avoid an eating disorder. The U.S. Department of Agriculture (USDA) can show people how. In 2005, the USDA updated its food pyramid to reflect the latest scientific information about the kinds of foods needed to maintain a healthy lifestyle.

According to its dietary guidelines, a healthy diet "emphasizes fruits, vegetables, whole grains, and fat-free or low-fat milk and milk products; includes lean meats, poultry, fish, beans, eggs, and nuts; and is low in saturated fats, trans fats, cholesterol, salt and added sugars."[16] These guidelines are for anyone over two years old.

The food pyramid can be found at the USDA Web site. The site also includes interactive tools so that people can personalize their own eating plans and track their progress. The tools give advice about selecting the right foods, balancing food with exercise, getting the most nutrition from foods, and staying within the calorie needs that are best for each individual.

The slogan of the food pyramid is "Steps to a healthier you," suggesting that taking small steps toward good health is the best way to go.

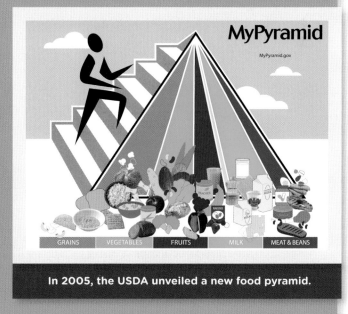

In 2005, the USDA unveiled a new food pyramid.

including making her feel tired, hungry, and depressed. The best way to get the body to the right weight is to do it slowly with healthy eating and regular exercise.

Not only do many Americans consider thinness beautiful, but they also consider being overweight ugly—and a reason to be ashamed. Some people even see it as a sign of laziness and lack of control. How many girls or women are willing to reveal their true weight? In 2005, supermodel Tyra Banks put on a "fat suit" that made her look as if she weighed 350 pounds. She was shocked by the reaction. People openly stared at her and even laughed in her face.[17]

Professor Bradley Greenberg, who researched the media's attitude toward overweight characters on prime-time television, says "the last socially acceptable prejudice is against fat people."[18] According to his study, overweight characters were less likely to date or have friends and more likely to be the object of a joke—all the more reason for people to want to be thin.

Not only do many Americans consider thinness beautiful, but they also consider being overweight ugly—and a reason to be ashamed.

Society's passion for thinness keeps growing. Mothers worry about being fat, sending subtle messages to their daughters that they should worry, too. Teens pressure their friends to drop a few pounds so they can be more attractive. Coaches convince young athletes that losing weight will help them win. Eating disorders will stay a problem as long as American culture values people for their physical appearance more than for their inner qualities.

Family Influence

Many people believe families are to blame for teens developing eating disorders. But families are just one more piece of the eating disorder puzzle. They are often not even aware of their influence. There are certain family types, however, that seem to be associated with eating disorders.[19] Teens in these families may mistake eating disorders for a solution to their problems. Instead, they end up creating even greater problems.

Some of the family types that can be associated with development of an eating disorder are the following:

- **"Perfect" families:** The emphasis is on perfection. Imperfection is considered a weakness and appearances are important. High achievement is expected. Stress is usually high. A teen may see anorexia as a way to fulfill her need for perfection, instead of developing a happier, more balanced way of living.

The pressure of a "perfect" family might influence the development of an eating disorder.

HOW REAL PEOPLE DEAL: REAL GIRLS HAVE CURVES

I t was always Kirsten Haglund's dream to be a ballerina. She admired older girls when they danced and noticed that they ate very little. Kirsten wanted to be just like them.

When she was fifteen, Kirsten began to exercise twice a day. Although she was naturally thin, she put herself on a starvation diet and eliminated sugar, fat, and carbohydrates. "If there was ever a situation where there was going to be food, like after church, I wouldn't go," she said.[20] It wasn't long before losing weight became an addiction.

Kirsten dropped twenty pounds. Then she attended a ballet camp for six weeks and lost another ten pounds. When her mother first saw Kirsten after the camp, she was so shaken that she rushed her to a doctor. Kirsten was diagnosed with anorexia.

But Kirsten couldn't see what was wrong. "I thought I was dieting," she said. "I was fine."[21] She wasn't fine, of course. She had a low heart rate, her circulation and kidneys were working poorly, and she was so thin that her collarbone stuck out. "I would feel fatigued walking up six stairs," she admitted.[22]

Kirsten immediately went into treatment with a therapist and a nutritionist. It took several months, but she was able to recover. She now exercises regularly and has a healthy attitude toward food. She decided to give up ballet, however. "I couldn't be in that world and be healthy," she said.[23]

What makes Kirsten's story unique? Three years after starting treatment, she was crowned Miss America for 2008. Overnight, she became a national role model for eating disorder awareness. During her one-year reign, she spoke often to girls about eating disorders, lobbied Congress about eating disorder issues, and gave interviews to the media, exposing the dangers of eating disorders.

Now Kirsten is proud of her body. "You have to have curves," she said. "You can't look like a stick-thin model."[24] But she still struggles with anorexia, describing it as a kind of addiction. She tries to be aware of the triggers and situations that can put her into an unhealthy frame of mind about weight.[25]

Kirsten hopes that her own story will inspire other girls to face their struggles with eating disorders. "I want them to see that to be successful, you don't have to be perfect," she said. "You don't have to be completely put together. You can have flaws, and you can be imperfect, and you can just be a normal girl."[26]

- **Enmeshed families:** Members are overly involved with each other. Family loyalty is essential. Boundaries can be fuzzy and privacy is often lacking. An eating disorder may become an unhealthy way for a teen to separate from parents and establish a personal identity.
- **Overprotective families:** Parents act as buffers between children and problems, offering them no experience at resolving conflict. Teens may feel smothered. An eating disorder might provide them with a temporary feeling of independence. In reality they become dependent on the disorder.
- **Chaotic families:** Crisis and conflict are everyday events. Parents offer little structure and guidance. Teens may feel torn between making their lives more predictable and being impulsive. Bulimia, which wavers between bingeing and purging, may feel comfortable to a teen in this situation. But it does not answer the real need for security and structure.

- **Disengaged families:** Intimacy is not encouraged. Feelings and problems are not discussed. Teens may feel lonely, confused, and abandoned. An eating disorder may comfort them or be a way to get their parents' attention, but it does not help them deal with their feelings.

Other family situations—marriage problems, divorce, domestic violence, and substance abuse—are common among people with eating disorders. It is important to note, however, that most people experience negative family issues without developing eating disorders.

Influence of Psychological or Personality Traits

Eating disorders cannot be blamed on culture and families alone. Some psychological traits make it more likely for a person to develop an eating disorder. In many ways, eating disorders are outward expressions of inner problems.

What does that mean? People with eating disorders usually have poor coping skills. Instead of dealing with problems, they use their disorders as a way to control, avoid, or distract themselves. In the case of bulimia, for instance, purging may be a way of expressing anger for having been abused.

In many ways, eating disorders are outward expressions of inner problems.

Here are some of the psychological or personality traits that are risk factors for eating disorders:

Poor self-esteem: People with poor self-esteem have little confidence in themselves. They struggle with life's setbacks, and it can affect their mood and relationships. They may either stop trying or act as if nothing is wrong. Poor self-esteem is often tied to body image. A poor body image can lead to eating disorders.

Low self-worth: Teens with low self-worth never feel sufficiently worthy. They believe they can achieve, but whatever they do is not good enough. As soon as one goal is reached, they look for another. As a result, they make unrealistic demands on themselves (like trying to look like a model).

Need for approval: People with poor self-esteem and low self-worth are usually desperate for approval from others because they cannot find it within. Giving others reason to admire them becomes their focus. If someone suggests they should lose weight to look better, they will do what it takes to satisfy them.

Need for control: Eating disorders give teens a feeling of control. A girl with anorexia may not be able to control her personal life, but she can control the amount of food that goes into her body. When a boy with bulimia purges, he may be showing his parents that they cannot control what he does with his food. In both cases, it is only the illusion of control. The eating disorders are really controlling them.

Depression: When people are depressed, they feel sad, discouraged, and hopeless. They tend to keep to themselves, sometimes stop eating, and may even be suicidal. It is a trait that goes hand in hand with eating disorders, both before and while they occur.

Anxiety: People who are anxious expect the worst, but their fears are usually irrational. Obsessive-compulsive disorder (OCD) is an anxiety disorder common in people with anorexia. Those with OCD think obsessively about something and have an intense need to repeat specific behaviors in a particular way to release tension. Eventually, the obsessive thoughts will not go away, even when the person realizes what they are, much as thoughts about food will not go away, even when people really want to recover from anorexia. For someone with anorexia, obsessing about a strict diet with lots of rules is the perfect way to satisfy that need.

Obsessive thinking: Who doesn't get a craving for a favorite food? Whether people are "chocoholics" or have a "sweet tooth," the more they deny their cravings, the more they think about them. Spending too much time thinking about food is obsessive. Some people are so obsessive they cannot resist the impulse to binge.

Black-and-white thinking: People who think in black and white see their bodies only as bad or good, fat or thin. There is no in-between. This kind of thinking can often lead to anorexia; people feel they are either successes or failures.

Perfectionist thinking: Perfectionists refuse to believe that anything short of perfect is acceptable. They tend to be critical of their own performance and believe if they do not do well they are worthless. Perfectionists are driven by both the need for approval and the fear of failure—which makes them "perfect" candidates for eating disorders.

Life Changes or Stressful Events

Life changes, such as moving, starting a new school, or ending a relationship can leave people with the feeling that their lives are out of control. An eating disorder gives people the mistaken impression there is something they *can* control—their eating. The eating disorder, of course, is really controlling them.

Teasing someone about their weight is more hurtful than people realize. In a study of 2,500 adolescents, girls who had been teased about their weight at the beginning of the study were more likely than their peers to become frequent dieters five years later. Boys who were teased were more likely to become binge eaters and have unhealthy weight control behaviors.[27]

Traumatic events can leave a person emotionally scarred for years. Memories of car crashes, hurricanes, fires, or suicides can bring up feelings of sadness or anger. An eating disorder can be a way for someone to hide from or express his pain—instead of dealing with it.

Sexual abuse during childhood is also a risk factor. People with anorexia admit using weight loss and starvation to avoid their own sexuality. In fact, anorexia actually slows down or halts puberty and normal development. People with bulimia describe purging as a way to make their insides clean and express anger at their abuser. Binge eaters who were abused say they numb themselves by overeating.[28]

Biology

Centuries ago, physicians believed that anorexia was a physical disorder that could be healed with medicines. After decades of focusing on cultural and psychological factors of eating disorders, research has turned once again to finding a biological solution to the problem.

Genes: Current research is examining the possibility that genes and chemicals in the brain have a significant effect on eating disorders. In fact, genes may be a greater factor in eating disorders than was once believed.

Genetics is a branch of biology that studies how people inherit certain characteristics, such as their eye color, from their parents. Recent studies have found that some people may also inherit a genetic predisposition (tendency) for eating disorders.

Eating disorders often run in families. In fact, relatives of people with eating disorders are at greater risk for developing a disorder themselves. People who have a sister or mother with anorexia are twelve times more likely to develop the disorder than people with no family history. They also have a four times greater risk for bulimia.[29]

The question is, what puts them at risk? Genetics or sharing the same environment? The answer is both. Recent studies with twins offer new insights on the subject. Here is how it works: Identical twins share the same genes and fraternal twins about half their genes, so disorders occurring more often in identical twins are believed to be genetic.

When it comes to the role of environment, it depends on what kind it is—shared or unique. A shared environment includes those aspects shared by both twins, such as social or economic status, religion, and parenting style. A unique environment—a trauma or involvement in a sport encouraging thinness—is experienced by only one twin.

These new studies have found that the effects of a unique environment are more significant than those of a shared environment. The studies also show that genetic background contributes substantially to eating disorders as well as to the psychological traits associated with them.[30]

After much searching, researchers believe they have found genes related to anorexia on chromosome 1.[31] A chromosome is a DNA strand that has hundreds or thousands of genes on it. Humans have 23 pairs of chromosomes and an estimated 35,000–50,000 genes. It will be difficult to find all the genes related to eating disorders.

According to Cynthia Bulik, a leading psychologist, researcher, and investigator of eating disorders, it is not likely that only one gene predisposes people to anorexia, but several of them.[32] This may include genes for anxiety, depression, or perfectionism—all psychological traits that put people at risk for anorexia.

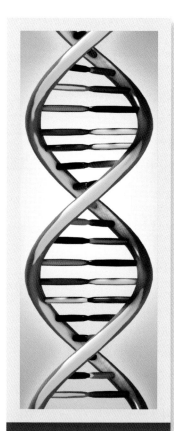

Genes on a person's DNA may make that individual more susceptible to an eating disorder.

According to Cynthia Bulik, a leading psychologist, researcher, and investigator of eating disorders, it is not likely that only one gene predisposes people to anorexia, but several of them.

Chemicals in the brain: Serotonin is a chemical that transmits messages between nerve cells in the brain. In humans it is involved in functions such as impulse control and appetite. Low levels of serotonin can cause depression and high levels can cause anxiety. Researchers found that people with anorexia and bulimia had abnormal levels of serotonin in their brains and concluded that abnormal serotonin levels may be a risk factor for eating disorders.[33]

Dopamine is another chemical that transmits messages between nerve cells. Disturbances in dopamine activity may contribute to weight changes, eating, and a sense of reward in anorexia. People with anorexia appear to have increased activity in their dopamine receptors. Since food stimulates the release of dopamine, it may explain why women with anorexia do not enjoy eating and why it takes so little to make them feel full.[34]

HOW CAN TEENS PREVENT EATING DISORDERS?

Right now some people are probably saying, "I'm just a teen. How can I prevent eating disorders?" Teens may not be able to get rid of the traits they inherited from their parents. They may not be able to change family dynamics or the culture in which they live. And they may not be able to resolve the genetic and chemical factors behind eating disorders—yet. But there *is* a lot teens can do to make a difference.

Get Educated About Eating Disorders
This book is a good place to start. A list of organizations with information about eating disorders can be found under "For More Information" at the end of this book. Suggested Internet addresses and a list of books are also included there. School and local libraries are usually good sources of information, too. The more people know about eating disorders, the easier it will be to prevent them.

Know the Media Is Not Always Right

People are not born wanting to be thin. They are taught to want it. The media often creates insecurities in people, then they target those insecurities to sell products. Accepting everything the media says as the truth is a mistake. People should always think for themselves instead.

SAY what

What Is Diabulimia?

Eating disorders are common in teenage girls and young women, and they are twice as common in those with type 1 diabetes. Why? People with diabetes have to follow strict food regimens to stay healthy. These regimens can lead girls to become obsessed with food which, in turn, can lead to an eating disorder.

A new kind of phenomenon, unofficially called diabulimia, has appeared among diabetics, who must take insulin several times a day to survive. People with diabulimia skip or restrict their insulin intake to lose weight. One study estimates that 30 percent of teen girls with type 1 diabetes have practiced this behavior.[35] Short-term effects are tiredness and muscle loss. Long-term effects can be devastating—blindness and heart or kidney disease.

Diabetics can lower their risk of developing an eating disorder by practicing a few simple behaviors:

- Focus on food *choices* rather than *restrictions*.
- Avoid talking about food as "good" or "bad."
- Replace boring exercises with fun recreational sports.
- Talk about feelings, especially when stressed.[36]

Diabetics face special challenges when it comes to eating disorders.

Build Self-Esteem

Self-criticism is a waste of time. Outer appearance should not define a person. Inner qualities are what count. Young people and adults who have poor self-esteem should make a list of their strengths and talents, celebrate their achievements, ask their friends for their positive reinforcement, and look for positive role models in their lives. They can think about who they spend their time with: friends who obsess over their looks

Can You Exercise Too Much?

Exercise should be part of any healthy lifestyle. It can help fight disease, make your heart and lungs stronger, and keep you at a healthy weight. People who exercise regularly live longer, feel better, and sleep more soundly. Besides, exercise is fun.

But exercise taken to the extreme is no fun at all. It can even hurt you. A common symptom of anorexia and bulimia is compulsive exercising. It happens when a person feels he *must* exercise and is guilty and anxious if he does not.

How much exercise is too much? The U.S. Food and Drug Administration recommends thirty minutes of physical activity a day for adults and sixty minutes for teens.[37] But compulsive exercisers work out several times a day and for up to five hours or more. They also tend to arrange their lives around exercising. Nothing—friends, sickness, or even bad weather—can stop them from working out.

Compulsive exercising can interfere with school, friendships, and work. It can also result in serious physical difficulties: stress fractures, dehydration, depression, heart problems, osteoporosis, arthritis, and reproductive issues. And it does not give the body enough time to heal between workouts, risking damage to muscles, tendons, ligaments, and joints.

So keep on exercising. Just don't overdo it.

and ask "Do I look fat?" over and over, or friends who are involved in lots of types of activities and support each other. Self-respect is the key to a happy and fulfilling life.

Learn to Admire Inner Qualities

Avoid prejudice toward people because of their weight, size, or body shape. Instead, look at their inner qualities, like kindness, honesty, patience, and humor. Make an effort to take people seriously, especially girls and women. Teasing others about their weight or making jokes at their expense is cruel—not funny.

Be Realistic

Nobody is perfect. Being unsuccessful at something does not mean failure. Know that everyone has special talents and abilities. Learn from mistakes (everyone makes them) and try again. Think of each challenge as a series of small steps forward. Pat yourself on the back along the way, and *never* put yourself down. It will only keep you from moving forward.

Focus on a Healthy Lifestyle

Resist the urge to diet or skip meals. Instead, develop healthy eating habits. The U.S. Department of Agriculture (USDA) has a Food Guide Pyramid that can help (see "What Is a Food Pyramid for Healthy Eating?" on page 63). Exercise regularly and have fun doing it. Take a walk, ride a bike, or go dancing. Learn how to get rid of stress. When things start to pile up, cut back a little. Try yoga, practice meditation, or have a good cry.

Communicate

Acknowledge real feelings honestly and talk about them with parents and friends who can be trusted. Keep a daily journal. People who write about what is going on in their lives are better able to keep in touch with what is going on in their heads. Be a good listener. Other people's feelings count, too.

Step Into the World
Make good use of strengths and talents by sharing them with the rest of the world. Take an art class, join a book club, or volunteer at a daycare center. Find a way to have fun and meet others with shared interests. Life has so much to offer.

Be a Role Model
Encourage friends to be themselves, too. Talk to them about the risks of eating disorders. Encourage them to seek help if they need it. If someone is making fun of a person's size or shape, ask him or her to stop. Let others know how much their friendship means.

WHAT CAN TEENS ASK PARENTS TO DO?

Get parents to help. Have a conversation about how the media influences eating disorders. Share your concerns about dieting and focusing too much on weight and shape. Encourage parents

Keeping a journal or diary can put teens in touch with their feelings about eating habits.

to live a healthy lifestyle, too. Ask them to insist on healthy food options for kids in school. Suggest they encourage school libraries to purchase books about nutrition and fitness. Write letters together demanding that politicians make educating kids and teens about eating disorders a priority.

If speaking out against the problem of eating disorders saves one person's life, it's worth it.

CHAPTER FIVE

Diagnosis and Treatment

A famous woman once said, "You can never be too rich or too thin."[1] It was Wallis Simpson, the duchess of Windsor and wife of the former king Edward VII of England. She said this at least fifty years ago, but many people believe it just as passionately today.

Of course, you *can* be too thin. But because our society equates beauty and self-worth with thinness, as many as 45 million Americans go on diets every year.[2] Unfortunately, most diets are unsuccessful, and people gain back the weight they lose.

Some diets, though, are too successful. In some people, diets trigger the desire to lose more and more weight. When this happens, people need help to stop their unhealthy, destructive behaviors.

Recovering from an eating disorder is hard, but it is not impossible. Admitting there is a problem is the first step. Then, it's important to gather family and friends around for support, and to see a doctor familiar with eating disorders. The earlier treatment starts, the better the chance of recovery and the less the chance of lasting physical effects. This chapter describes medical and psychological assessments used to diagnose eating disorders and the treatments used to restore healthy bodies and healthy minds.

TAKING THE FIRST STEP

Starving, bingeing, purging, and other unhealthy behaviors serve a vital purpose in the lives of people with eating disorders. Such behaviors calm them, make them feel safe and in control,

Recovery from an eating disorder can be made easier with help from specialists.

numb emotional pain, and allow them to punish themselves, release anger, or get attention. Admitting they have a problem and need help is terrifying. It feels like going rock climbing, but having your rope and harness yanked away unexpectedly.

This fear makes people with eating disorders put up walls when friends and family members try to help. Concerned people should not give up, but should avoid coming on too strong. Trying to understand how people with eating disorders feel and accepting them for who they are helps open the lines of communication.

Sometimes, parents have to force a young person to go for treatment. Even adults have to be forced to go for treatment, especially when an eating disorder becomes life-threatening. With adults, this is usually accomplished by staging an intervention. With a therapist or other professional present, the person with the eating disorder is confronted by family members and friends. Then the problem is discussed, and the person usually has little choice but to accept (and get) help.

Even adults have to be forced to go for treatment, especially when an eating disorder becomes life-threatening.

Once a person agrees to get help, friends and family members must act fast. They should be ready with information on eating disorders specialists and treatment programs. It's also important that they get treatment started immediately, before the person changes her mind or gets any sicker.

SETTING GOALS

Professionals who treat eating disorders set several goals for patients. Here are some important ones:

- Gaining back the weight lost from dieting and purging (in anorexia)
- Halting purging behaviors, such as vomiting, abuse of laxatives and diuretics, and excessive exercising (in anorexia and bulimia)
- Halting binge eating (in bulimia and binge-eating disorders)
- Teaching healthy eating and exercise behaviors (in all eating disorders)
- Resolving the psychological problems that contributed to (or caused) the eating disorder, such as low self-worth, poor self-esteem, distorted body image, and problems expressing anger (in all eating disorders)
- Reaching full recovery or, at least, a significant improvement (in all eating disorders).[3, 4]

WORKING AS A TEAM

Before treatment, people with eating disorders feel isolated and lonely. But once they start treatment, they have plenty of company. It takes a whole team of health professionals to help patients get well.

Members of the treatment team may include a family practitioner or pediatrician as well as doctors in various specialties, including a psychiatrist, a nutritionist, and a therapist. Working together, they design a treatment plan for each patient, taking into account age, overall health, family situation, type of eating disorder, and many other factors. This teamwork is called a "multidisciplinary approach."

The professionals who treat eating disorders will set and explain important goals for the patient.

HOW REAL PEOPLE DEAL: RISKING HIS LIFE TO MAKE WEIGHT

Shane Sellers was one of the most successful jockeys of all time. During his 26-year career, he rode in 14 Kentucky Derbies and won more than 4,000 races. But his success came at a terrible price.

Horseracing is a dangerous sport, and many jockeys get seriously injured. What most people do not realize is that jockeys risk their lives even before they get on a horse. They cannot race unless they "make weight," and they can kill themselves trying to do so.

"In the morning, I would get up and take a diet pill, drink a cup of coffee," Shane said. "I went to bed with nothing in my stomach, either. Maybe, you know, just a piece of ham."[5]

Racetracks set limits on how much weight a horse can carry. Usually, it is between 112 and 126 pounds, including the saddle and other gear. So jockeys have to weigh around 110 pounds. Shane was only 5 feet 3 inches tall, but his natural weight was about 150 pounds. To get down to 110, he took drastic measures. Most jockeys do.

Besides diet pills and starving, Shane spent about two hours every day in a sauna, called a "hot box" in jockey lingo. There, he would "pull four or five pounds of water," more jockey lingo for sweating off pounds.[6] Afterward, he would be weak and dehydrated.

Hot boxes can be found in most jockey locker rooms. Also found there are special toilets used just for "heaving" or "flipping" (both terms are slang for throwing up). Jockeys often force themselves to vomit to make weight.

"I was heaving three or five to six, seven times a day," Shane admitted.[18] Sometimes, he would get so hungry he would eat huge amounts of food and then heave. He got so good at it, he did not even have to stick his finger down his throat.

On top of all this, Shane took diuretics and ran for hours dressed in layers of clothes to increase sweating. Afterward, he had his wife wrap him in blankets so he would sweat even more.

Often, Shane was so dizzy that he saw spots while he was racing and so weak that he could not stop the horse on his own. He was a frail 110-pound man on a 1,000-pound horse.

Doctors warned him that he was killing himself. But racing was in his blood, and he kept on until a serious knee injury forced him to retire in 2004. Devastated, he sought help from a therapist, who prescribed antidepressants. Today, Shane weighs a healthy 150 pounds and exercises normally. And for the first time in more than twenty years, he enjoys food.

He still loves horses, but now he breeds and trains them at his farm in Louisiana. He has also written an autobiography called *Freedom's Rein* and works hard to improve the lives of jockeys by discussing the need to get weight limits raised so the number of eating disorders will decrease.

"I don't want to be remembered for what I did on the racetrack," Shane said. "I was no better than the next guy. I want to be remembered as somebody that made a change in this industry for the better, for riders."[7]

The patient's first appointment is usually with a family practitioner or a pediatrician. Family practitioners are doctors who treat patients of all ages. Pediatricians treat patients from infancy to age eighteen. If the patient has complications from the eating disorder, the doctor will refer the patient to a specialist.

The doctor may also refer the patient to a nutritionist—an expert on teaching healthy eating habits and dealing with nutrition problems. Two other important referrals are to a therapist and a psychiatrist, who are both trained to treat psychological problems. A psychiatrist has a medical degree and may prescribe medication, which is often used in treating eating disorders.

All of these health professionals must have experience in treating eating disorders; otherwise, treatment probably will not be successful. Before making that first appointment, a person should ask the doctor about his or her experience. Doctors not skilled in treating eating disorders probably know other doctors who are experienced and can recommend them. Other ways to find a doctor include asking a trusted family member or friend, calling a hospital, looking in the phone book's yellow pages under "eating disorders," or searching the Internet (see "For More Information" at the end of this book).

MEDICAL ASSESSMENT

Making a first appointment and talking honestly about an eating disorder takes courage. Children will need a parent present during the exam to help answer questions. Teens and even adults may feel more at ease with a parent or caring friend present for support.

Patient History

The family practitioner or pediatrician will start the exam by asking a lot of questions. This is called the patient history and provides important background information. The doctor will ask about the patient's eating habits, general health, and psychological health. Here are some typical questions:

- What do you eat every day?
- How much?
- Do you have food cravings?
- Do you wake up at night and eat?
- Do you vomit, use laxatives, or take diuretics?
- Are you constipated, bloated?

- Have you stopped getting periods?
- Does your heart pound?
- Do you cry often?
- Do you worry about germs and wash your hands frequently?

What Is an Assessment?

An assessment is the process a doctor goes through to arrive at a diagnosis for a patient. Also called an evaluation, it involves subjective (personal) findings based on the patient's answers to questions about his illness. It also includes objective (observable) findings based on the physical examination, medical tests, and data from family members and other health professionals. Put together, this information forms the basis for the doctor's diagnosis. Diagnosing an eating disorder requires assessments from both a doctor and a therapist.

Doctors combine objective and subjective findings to arrive at an assessment of the patient.

Patients Must Live Away From Home During Treatment

Not true. Most people with eating disorders are outpatients—they live at home and keep attending school, working, or caring for their families. They see a therapist once or twice a week and also continue seeing their medical doctor and nutritionist. These professionals usually have offices at an eating disorders clinic or mental health clinic. Outpatient treatment allows patients to set their own schedule and be more flexible.

Inpatient treatment involves checking into a hospital or live-in treatment center. Many people do this to beat eating disorders, as well as alcoholism and drug addiction. These facilities provide twenty-four-hour care and have a staff of doctors, nurses, therapists, and nutritionists. Inpatient treatment offers the advantage of constant supervision. Patients can concentrate on getting well and are less likely to revert to old behaviors. Unfortunately, these facilities are very expensive and health insurance often will not pay for them.

People with eating disorders whose lives are in danger require inpatient treatment.

Who needs inpatient care? Anyone whose life is in danger. Candidates include anorexia sufferers who have irregular heartbeats or who need tube feedings; bulimia sufferers who binge and purge so often they vomit blood, who cannot keep their medicine down, or who have dehydration and electrolyte imbalances; and anyone who is suicidal. People with binge-eating disorder may also become inpatients because of complications of obesity, such as high blood pressure and diabetes.

Physical Examination, Diagnosis, and Tests

After the patient history, the doctor will perform a physical exam. This includes checking weight, height, and body mass index, listening to the heart and lungs with a stethoscope, recording temperature, pulse, and blood pressure, and examining the body from head to toe. He will note thinning hair, brittle nails, dry skin, lanugo hair, dental problems, or callused knuckles, which are signs of eating disorders.

The doctor does not usually diagnose an eating disorder; this is usually done by a psychiatrist or psychologist. Eating disorders cannot be detected by a blood test, X-ray, or other procedure. However, the doctor will order these types of tests to make sure the patient's symptoms are not caused by cancer, thyroid problems, or another illness. If the patient is later diagnosed with an eating disorder, these tests can also reveal its impact on the body.

The remainder of this chapter covers testing and treatment for anorexia, bulimia, binge-eating disorder, and eating disorders not otherwise specified (EDNOS) that are similar to these three illnesses.

PSYCHOLOGICAL ASSESSMENT

After the family practitioner or pediatrician gathers the basic facts, a therapist does a psychological examination to obtain a more complete picture of the patient and the eating disorder. Therapists also take a patient history, but their questions are much more detailed and may take place over several sessions. To save time, therapists may have patients fill out history questionnaires at home.

A psychological exam is essentially the same for all types of eating disorders. The therapist will refer to the doctor's medical findings, but will still ask some medical questions, especially if the patient has left out important facts.

The Eating Disorder Examination is the best method for collecting information on eating disorders and diagnosing them.

In this exam, the therapist asks the patient questions about eating habits and feelings about shape and weight. The therapist may also ask about the patient's reasons for seeking treatment, family relationships, and family exercise and eating habits, as well as the patient's support systems and goals for weight and recovery. Other questions involve asking about anxiety or depression, past or current substance abuse, and physical or sexual abuse. Finally, the therapist finds out how much the

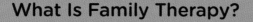

What Is Family Therapy?

Eating disorders can have a negative impact on the lives of all family members, not just the person suffering from the disorder. By the same token, what happens in families (family patterns or behaviors) can have a negative impact, too; in many cases, families can cause or contribute to eating disorders. For this reason, including families in therapy sessions is essential to the patient's recovery.

For children, teens, and young adults, family therapy may include parents and siblings. For older adults, it may include just the patient's spouse. Family therapy can also be done in groups, with several families present. In all cases, it helps people communicate, examine relationships, resolve family conflicts, and pinpoint attitudes, behaviors, and events that may have contributed to the eating disorder.

During therapy, family members learn to understand the eating disorder and how the patient feels, so they can offer the right kind of support. The therapist also helps them set realistic goals for the patient's recovery, including weight goals. In a nutshell, the goal of therapy is to make the family realize that everyone in the house needs to change behaviors, *not just the patient*.

Another type of family therapy, called family-based therapy, takes place mainly at home with parents taking an extremely active role. This therapy is described in more detail in Chapter 6.

patient understands about her eating disorder and how motivated she is to overcome it.

Once the question-and-answer period is over, the therapist administers some written or oral tests. Two of these include the Eating Disorder Inventory and the Eating Attitudes Test. These tests ask questions about a person's eating habits and how they feel about food. Other tests measure how motivated a person is to change eating behaviors, how much body image means to them, and whether they have depression, anxiety, or other psychological problems.

The flaw in these tests is that patients may not be truthful when answering questions. In spite of this, psychological tests can provide useful insights when combined with all the other data gathered about the patient.[8]

NUTRITIONAL ASSESSMENT

Usually, patients are also assessed by a nutritionist, also called a dietician. A nutritionist asks specific questions about the patient's diet, such as past and present eating habits, feelings about food, eating-disorder behaviors such as bingeing or vomiting, and the impact the eating disorder has had on the patient's life. The nutritionist then shares this information with the doctor and therapist.

TREATING EATING DISORDERS

Once the assessments are over, the real work begins. Now, the doctor or doctors, therapist, nutritionist, patient, and patient's family can join forces to help the patient get healthy again. A psychiatrist may also evaluate the patient and prescribe medication.

Many people with eating disorders do well with carefully supervised outpatient therapy. But some acutely ill people need inpatient treatment for several weeks or months. Treatments for anorexia, bulimia, and binge-eating disorder share many common features. But each type of disorder also has unique features that require special treatment. Treatment for EDNOS depends on the patient's symptoms. For example, patients with EDNOS that resemble anorexia or bulimia are treated as if they had those disorders.

Many people with eating disorders do well with carefully supervised outpatient therapy. But some acutely ill people need inpatient treatment for several weeks or months.

Medical Treatment for Anorexia

With anorexia, the doctors' goals are to help patients get back to a healthy weight and prevent or treat complications. Severely emaciated patients may need to be hospitalized and receive tube feedings until they regain some weight. They may also need hospital treatment for complications, such as irregular heart rate, low blood pressure, abnormal electrolyte levels, and low bone density (osteoporosis).

Once patients get closer to ideal weight, most complications go away. However, osteoporosis may be permanent. Bone density is the amount of mineral in bone that makes it solid and strong. In females, low body weight and lack of body fat can cause the sex hormone estrogen to become ineffective so menstrual periods stop (a condition called amenorrhea). In males, low body weight and low body fat can decrease the sex hormone

A physical examination is one part of treatment for an eating disorder.

Bone Density Tests

Bone density is measured with a test called dual-energy X-ray absorptiometry, or DXA scan for short. The test uses only one-tenth the radiation of a chest X-ray. The most accurate scans are performed on the lower spine and hip.

Patients must go to a doctor's office or hospital outpatient department to have a DXA scan. They can eat normally, but should stop taking calcium pills at least twenty-four hours prior to the test. Undressing is usually not necessary, but patients should not wear jewelry or clothes that have zippers or contain other metal. They will also be asked to remove keys, wallets, and other items from their pockets. X-rays can damage an unborn baby, so women should not have this test if they are pregnant or think they might be.

During the test, the patient lies on a cushioned table. An X-ray scanner located above the table is passed over the body. A computer monitor shows images of bone. The test is painless, but patients must stay very still and may be asked to hold their breath for a few seconds to keep the X-ray image from blurring. The entire test only takes about ten minutes.

A doctor called a radiologist interprets the results and decides whether there is bone loss and if so, how much. Test results are recorded as T-scores and Z-scores. The T-score compares a patient's bone density to a healthy young person's. The Z-score compares it to other healthy patients of the same age, race, and gender as the patient. A negative T- or Z-score (such as -1.8) means that bones are thinner and more brittle than is considered healthy. The lower the negative score, the thinner the bones.

Many people with anorexia who are between the ages of twenty and twenty-five have been found to have bone densities similar to people aged seventy or eighty. Seeing evidence of osteoporosis can be a wake-up call for people with anorexia.[9]

testosterone, causing a low or absent sex drive. All of these factors contribute to a decrease in bone density, which raises the risk of broken bones.

Osteoporosis usually occurs in middle-aged and elderly women. Their estrogen levels plunge after menopause, when menstruation stops permanently. Bone growth reaches peak levels during the teenage years, and if an eating disorder interrupts this growth, the outcome can be serious and permanent. Exercise, calcium pills with vitamin D, and possibly a medication to enhance calcium absorption and bone growth are all part of the mix. Both males and females with anorexia should have a bone density test to determine if they have osteoporosis.

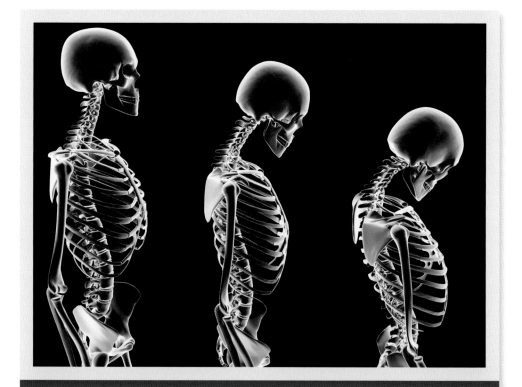

This artist rendition based on X-rays shows the curvature of the spine that can sometimes occur from severe osteoporosis, in which decreased density of bone mass creates bone fragility. Anorexia, which causes poor nutrition and improper mineral absorption, can contribute greatly to the development of osteoporosis.

Several drugs have been tested to determine if they will help patients with anorexia gain weight, have a realistic body image, and feel less anxious and depressed. So far, none has proven very effective. However, Zyprexa shows promise. An antipsychotic drug usually used to treat severe mental disorders, Zyprexa increases appetite, causes weight gain, and decreases anxiety and depression in some patients.[10]

Medical Treatment for Bulimia

Doctors' goals for bulimia are to prevent or correct any complications and stop purging behaviors. People with bulimia may need hospitalization to treat complications related to purging, such as anemia, severe electrolyte imbalance, and damage to the esophagus. Because purging is difficult to continue in the hospital, spending time there is a small step in the right direction.

Women with bulimia may also have osteoporosis and need treatment. This is especially true of those with non-purging bulimia, those who restrict food, exercise excessively, and often stop menstruating because of very low body fat levels. Studies have shown that people with bulimia who had anorexia in the past also have a higher risk of developing osteoporosis.[11]

Medications are much more successful in treating bulimia than anorexia. The antidepressant Luvox is often prescribed, because it helps prevent some patients from relapsing and quitting treatment. However, antidepressant use is controversial in teens and young adults, because these drugs increase the risk of suicidal thoughts.

Other medications for bulimia include Topamax, which is generally used to prevent seizures in epilepsy. Topamax has been successful in reducing bingeing and purging. However, it can also cause weight loss, so it should not be given to patients with low or even normal body weight.

The SCOFF Test

This quick-and-easy test can help identify people with anorexia or bulimia. It was developed in 1999 by researchers at St. George's Hospital Medical School in London and tested on more than two hundred women. The test detected 100 percent of the women who had anorexia and bulimia. Two "yes" answers indicate the test-taker may have anorexia or bulimia. One "yes" answer means the test-taker may have food or body image issues. Although reliable, this test is not meant to diagnose an eating disorder, but it may warn people that they need to get professional help.

Answer yes or no:

1. Do you make yourself **S**ick because you feel uncomfortably full?
2. Do you worry you have lost **C**ontrol over how much you eat?
3. Have you recently lost more than **O**ne stone (fourteen pounds) in a three-month period?
4. Do you believe yourself to be **F**at when others say you are too thin?
5. Would you say that **F**ood dominates your life?[12]

Prescription medications called antidepressants have been successful in treating bulimia.

Antiemetics—drugs that discourage vomiting—are sometimes used in the first few weeks of bulimia treatment. Medications that treat depression and reduce bingeing and purging may take a few weeks to become effective. Once these drugs start working, antiemetics are discontinued.

One last medical treatment for bulimia is phototherapy.

The patient is exposed to high-intensity light for thirty minutes to two hours per day. This special lighting is as intense as sunlight and is believed to increase the function of serotonin—a chemical in the brain that controls mood. Phototherapy can help patients feel less depressed and anxious and less apt to binge or purge. Drugs for depression also affect serotonin levels.

Medical Treatment for Binge-Eating Disorder

Most people with binge-eating disorder are overweight or obese, so the doctor's goal is to treat complications related to bingeing and obesity. Some patients may need to be hospitalized at first for high blood pressure, diabetes, heart disease, or other obesity-related problems. Like patients with bulimia who cannot purge while in the hospital, binge eaters cannot overeat. So hospitalization can be a small step toward healthy eating.

Weight loss seems like a logical goal for overweight binge eaters. It is—but not at first. Before dieting can be successful, the reasons for binge eating must be explored and psychological problems successfully treated through therapy. Without therapy, dieting will not work. It might even set off more binge-eating behavior.[13]

Antidepressants like Prozac and Luvox are used to discourage bingeing in this disorder, as well as in bulimia. These drugs affect the serotonin levels in the brain that regulate when one feels full. One theory is that people with binge-eating syndrome do not have enough serotonin, so they do not recognize when they are full. However, even though patients do not binge as much, they do not lose weight while on these drugs.

Meridia is a new anti-obesity drug that has shown promising results. It curbs hunger and provides a feeling of fullness. Unfortunately, it can cause serious side effects, including high blood pressure and suicidal thoughts. Some studies also show that Topamax reduces binge eating.

Nutritional Treatment for Eating Disorders

The American Psychiatric Association lists nutritional rehabilitation as one of the chief goals in anorexia treatment.[14] But it is an important goal in treating *all* eating disorders. Sometimes, the therapist or doctor may try nutritional counseling, but this can backfire. Even though patients with eating disorders ignore all the rules of healthy eating, they feel they are "experts" on calories, weight loss, and nutrition. Having a qualified nutritionist handle food issues avoids the embarrassing problem of the student knowing more than the teacher!

No matter what the eating disorder, the nutritionist's goal is to teach patients that food is their friend, not their enemy. They do this by being frank about the deadly complications of eating disorders, encouraging patients to discuss their feelings, and having them keep food journals. A nutritionist can win the trust of patients, and teach them how to listen to their bodies and know when they are hungry and full. This is called intuitive eating, and it can take a long time to master. Just eating three meals a day is a huge milestone for most patients.

Nutritionists can help patients with eating disorders to identify "good" foods that are healthy to eat, like tomatoes and cucumbers.

No matter what the eating disorder, the nutritionist's goal is to teach patients that food is their friend, not their enemy.

What Nutritionists Do

Nutritionists do much more than tell people what to eat. A nutritionist who works with people who are recovering from eating disorders can do all of the following:

- Present the hard facts about what eating disorders do to the body.
- Help banish mistaken beliefs about food and stop food rituals.
- Slowly reintroduce into the patient's diet "bad" foods, "scary" foods, or foods that have triggered binges.
- Do not insist that patients gain a certain amount of weight in a certain time. One to two pounds a week is a realistic goal.
- Avoid discussing weight or calories unless absolutely necessary.
- Use meal plans if the patient needs them, but do not make them a requirement for every patient.
- Stress that change will not happen overnight and setbacks will occur.
- Involve the family in therapy by teaching them about healthy eating.
- Keep the rest of the treatment team up to date on the patient's progress.
- Tell patients how much weight they have gained, not how much they actually weigh. Try to break their habit of constant weighing.
- Set goals for changing unhealthy behaviors and gaining weight. Use a range, not a specific number for weight goals. In anorexia, aim for 90 to 100 percent of the patient's ideal body weight and an 18 to 25 point BMI.[15]

Psychological Treatment for Eating Disorders

Talking about their problems with a therapist helps people with all types of eating disorders. Psychotherapy—also called talk therapy or counseling—has a proven track record and no harmful side effects like medications. But not all people can start it right away. Some people need to be hospitalized first. These include anorexia sufferers near starvation, those constantly bingeing and purging, those with serious medical complications, and those with suicidal tendencies. When life-threatening problems are resolved, people are strong enough physically and emotionally to benefit from psychotherapy.

Psychotherapy is not what people once saw in old black-and-white movies. The patient does not lie on a couch while a bearded therapist in a white lab coat takes notes behind the patient. During individual therapy, the patient meets privately with the therapist and they both sit comfortably facing each other. During group therapy, a therapist heads a discussion group of several patients with similar eating disorders. During family therapy, the therapist meets with patients and members of their families. With older patients, this may mean a husband or wife.

There are several approaches used in individual and group therapy. Therapists often combine them to suit particular patients. The most common approaches are described below.

Cognitive behavioral therapy: The philosophy behind this therapy is that changing how people think will help change how they behave. People with eating disorders are taught to replace negative thoughts about food and body image with positive thoughts. This helps prevent the irrational thinking common in eating disorders. One example is all-or-nothing thinking. ("I ate one cookie and blew my diet, so I might as well eat the whole box.") Another example is magical thinking. ("If I lose twenty pounds, all my problems will be solved.")

Studies show that this type of therapy helps in bulimia, binge-eating disorder, and EDNOS. Its usefulness in anorexia has not been proven. In a 2008 British study, 154 patients with bulimia and EDNOS who were not extremely under-weight had cognitive behavioral therapy once a week for 20 weeks. Fifteen months later, 61.4 percent of those with bulimia and 45.7 percent of those with EDNOS were still eating normally.[16]

Interpersonal therapy: This type of therapy deals with how eating disorders are connected to relationship issues. It does not involve discussions of food, weight, or body image. Many life experiences affect eating behavior, and patients are taught how to handle them. For example, eating disorders may be triggered by a death in the family, by moving to a new town or going away to college, or by getting married or getting a divorce. Learning to express feelings and deal with change in a healthy way (not by bingeing or starving) is the goal of interpersonal therapy.

Interpersonal therapy has been successful in anorexia, bulimia, and binge-eating disorder. In a 2002 study of 162 overweight people with binge-eating disorder, half received cognitive behavioral therapy and half received interpersonal therapy for twenty weeks. At the end of treatment, about 75 percent of people in both groups had recovered. One year later, recovery rates were still similar (about 60 percent each). However, neither type of therapy caused major weight loss.[17]

Dialectical behaviorial therapy: This approach combines cognitive behavioral and interpersonal therapy techniques. It is usually conducted in a group and helps teach patients how to curb harmful, impulsive behaviors and find ways of coping with stress that do not involve food. Four coping strategies are taught:

- **Mindfulness:** Being more aware of your feelings, reflecting and observing, and not reacting emotionally
- **Distress tolerance:** Finding healthy ways to deal with painful emotions
- **Interpersonal effectiveness:** Fostering successful relationships, including with yourself
- **Emotional regulation:** Experiencing emotions without having to react to them

Not much research has been done on dialectical behavioral therapy, but it appears to work well with both bulimia and binge-eating disorder.

A Few Words About Weight Loss Programs

Most people with binge-eating disorder who are obese need to lose weight for health reasons. When these people start treatment for eating disorders, they may ask if the therapist or nutritionist can put them on a diet. Many times, the answer is "no."

Why? Because undergoing treatment for an eating disorder is time-consuming and emotionally challenging. The patient has plenty to deal with, without trying to diet, too. Some therapists believe that low-calorie diets make people feel deprived and can set off episodes of binge eating. They deemphasize calories and try to lure people away from the bathroom scale. They believe that losing weight should come later, after the patient recovers from binge-eating disorder.

Some studies support this idea, but others do not. The American Psychiatric Association (APA) reports that "binge eating is substantially reduced in programs using very-low-calorie diets, but a small number of individuals may experience a reemergence of binge eating when regular meals are reintroduced."[18]

In addition, the APA reports that eating disorder therapy without weight control does not result in weight reduction. However, adding exercise improves weight loss and decreases bingeing. In the end, most people with binge-eating disorder regain weight after losing it, regardless of whether they received treatment.[19]

The bottom line? Experts are still debating the best ways to treat eating disorders. But remember: Doctors and other professionals did not recognize eating disorders as mental illnesses until 1980. Given this, we have actually come a long way in a relatively short time. Even so, much more research needs to be done.

CHAPTER SIX

Outlook for the Future

Not too long ago, eating disorders were thought of as a matter of choice, influenced by the idea that thin is beautiful. Now people know better. Today's understanding of eating disorders includes psychology, genetics, and the nervous system. The field is better organized, new medicines are proving effective, therapies seem to be working, and research has grown more complex. The advances are impressive—and yet, so much more work needs to be done.

Millions of people are still struggling with eating disorders. Some do not make it. The death rate from anorexia ranges from 10 to 20 percent. The suicide rate for women with eating disorders is 58 percent greater than the norm. Making therapy more accessible would help. The recovery rate for people with anorexia is 50 percent. The recovery rate for women with bulimia is 80 percent, *if* they are treated within the first five years.[1, 2]

Even though effective therapies are available, only one in ten patients takes advantage of it.[3] Inpatient treatment can cost $30,000 a month or more. Outpatient treatment can have a price tag of $100,000 over the length of an illness.[4] Many patients are unable to afford it. Either they have no insurance or their insurance will not cover eating disorders. When insurance does cover an eating disorder, the patient is often discharged before he or she has fully recovered. Although there are therapists who will work with a patient's financial situation to ensure necessary treatment, many patients do not take advantage of it. Another problem is that funding for eating disorders is inadequate. The Eating Disorders

Coalition for Research (EDC), estimates that the federal government is spending only $21 million a year on eating disorder research.[5] More money is needed, and not just for research. Doctors and other health professionals need training to recognize and treat eating disorders. Parents need to understand the symptoms and how they can help. Support groups are needed, especially for teens and children.

Unfortunately, many insurance policies do not cover all the costs of treatment for eating disorders.

Even though effective therapies are available, only one in ten patients takes advantage of it.

Public information on the subject is lacking. Doctors are not required to report patients with eating disorders to the department of public health, so statistics are unreliable. Schools spend twice as much time on alcohol and drug education as they do on eating disorder education. However, a study of middle schools and high schools in fifteen states found almost as many female students with eating disorders as total students with drug or alcohol problems.[6]

RAISING AWARENESS

Still, there is good news for the future of eating disorders. Several organizations have been working together to raise awareness of the problem on a state, federal, and international level. Their goals are the same: to educate people about eating disorders, to help those who suffer from these illnesses, and to encourage needed research so that eating disorders can be prevented in the future.

On a National Level

The EDC was founded in 2000 "to advance the federal recognition of eating disorders as a public health priority." By educating lawmakers and the public about the risks of eating disorders, the EDC hopes to achieve:

- Better resources for education and prevention
- More funding for scientific research
- Improved training programs for professionals
- Better access to patient care
- Supportive programs for the development of children's health
- More citizens to advocate for people with eating disorders[7]

The EDC has succeeded in bringing federal attention to the eating disorder problem, but only one bill it supported has become law—the Mental Health Parity and Addiction Equity Act passed by Congress in 2008. (Parity means a state of being equal or equivalent.) It was a much-needed step in the right direction.

Here is a little background: Insurance companies have a history of not covering physical and mental illnesses equally. In 2007, only twenty-six states included serious mental illness in their parity laws and only twenty states included eating disorders.[8] This makes it hard on people with eating disorders who have had to settle for less than adequate coverage for treatment.

The new parity law now requires insurance companies to give Americans with mental health and substance abuse conditions the same coverage as they would for physical illnesses. There is just one hitch. Although eating disorders are officially considered mental illnesses, the bill does not mention them specifically. That means people who need insurance should check their state laws and their insurance rules to see what is covered and for how long. Meanwhile, the EDC will continue to work to make sure eating disorders get the same benefits as other mental illnesses.

College Students Have a Higher Risk for Eating Disorders

Sad, but true. When the NEDA did a survey of more than 1,000 college students in 2006, almost 20 percent admitted to having experienced an eating disorder at some time. There was an even more chilling fact. From that group, 75 percent had never gone for treatment.[9]

Eating disorders occur at different developmental stages of life, and college is a major one. The stress of leaving their families may overwhelm some students. Add the pressure of making new friends and taking on a full course load, and some of them develop eating disorders to deal with their anxiety.

The stress of college life can trigger an eating disorder.

Some colleges tackle the problem by offering counseling and support groups. In 2009, 470 college campuses were registered with the National Eating Disorders Screening Program, a non-profit organization that screens college students for eating disorders, provides them with educational materials, and connects at-risk students with the help they need.[10]

HOW REAL PEOPLE DEAL: THE GIRL WHO HAD IT ALL

n high school, Amy had it all—a cool boyfriend, near perfect grades, the lead in the school play, and a position as editor on the school paper. She loved to paint, won several art awards, and planned to study art in college. Amy wanted to do it all, but by the beginning of senior year, she was burnt out.

At home, things were difficult. Her parents fought often, and her dad seemed to ignore her, except when he was angry at something she did. She was too upset by her parents' bickering to eat dinner at home and was usually too busy to eat at school. That was how she started to lose weight.

Amy didn't realize she had lost weight until her friends and family—especially her dad—started complimenting her on how she looked. It made her feel good, so she began to try to lose weight. She ate only low-fat foods and became a vegetarian. Her clothes were soon hanging off her.

When her mother said she was worried about how much weight Amy had lost, Amy brushed it off. She hated to admit that she had not eaten properly for months, so she pretended she had a flu that would not go away. She knew about the dangers of anorexia, but she never saw her weight loss as a warning sign. Amy was in denial.

By the second semester, Amy was exhausted. She hardly had enough energy to keep up with her artwork. Everything took so much effort. By now, she was only having an apple and some water at every meal. When her friends begged her to eat, she refused. It gave her a feeling of power to ignore them and starve herself. But Amy was no longer happy.

"Having an eating disorder is so lonely—losing weight is the only thing that really matters. I forgot . . . my passions and interests, friends, and family. All I had was the ability to make myself sicker."[11]

When Amy went off to college she weighed about ninety pounds. She still would not admit how sick she was—even to herself. But it affected her more and more.

"I couldn't concentrate on lectures. I couldn't remember a thing I had read moments after reading it. Just climbing a set of stairs made my heart race. I was always exhausted. I didn't even want to paint."[12]

One day a stranger told her she had better take care of herself, and Amy broke down. She called her parents and asked them to pick her up. She felt like a failure.

Amy's parents brought her to a center that treated people with eating disorders. Her first days were difficult. She had been lying to herself for months and now she had to see a therapist every day and be honest and open about her illness. At mealtimes, she was supposed to eat everything on her plate.

"I wanted to eat, but I couldn't. My body wasn't used to eating and it was incredibly difficult. Food came back up my throat right after I swallowed."[13]

But Amy forced herself to eat and eventually she could keep her food down. She began to feel better. She also spent time in group therapy. Confiding in other people who were going through the same experience helped her to heal, too.

Amy's parents also got counseling at the center. One day her father told her, "You don't have to be sick for me to notice you," and asked her to forgive him.[14] Amy began to realize that anorexia may have been her way of getting the attention she craved from her dad.

Amy is now in recovery. She feels better physically and hopes she did not damage her body too badly. She sometimes gets anxious about gaining weight, but she is trying to change that. Instead she says, "I deserve to take up space and make a place for myself."[15] Meanwhile, she is taking small steps toward her future.

"So far, my life has not turned out at all as I expected. But I'm tons stronger than I thought I was. And I know it's OK, even necessary, to ask for help when you're struggling."[16]

In 2009, the EDC also lobbied for the following legislation:

- The FREED Act (the Federal Response to Eliminate Eating Disorders), a bill that addresses eating disorders among the general public, including research, treatment, education, and prevention.
- The IMPACT Act, which approaches the prevention of obesity together with the prevention of eating disorders, recognizing that the two problems are interdependent.
- The Eating Disorders Awareness, Prevention, and Education Act, which plans to raise awareness of eating disorders in schools and create educational programs to prevent them.

On an International Scale

At an international conference in 2006, the Academy for Eating Disorders (AED) launched a Worldwide Charter for Action on Eating Disorders. The purpose of the charter was to give people tools to help them identify high-quality and appropriate practices, and to avoid outdated practices.

At the Grassroots Level

To bring better awareness of eating disorders to the state level, the NEDA initiated a new program in 2009 called STAR (States for Treatment, Access, and Research). The STAR program hopes to improve access to eating disorder treatment by enlisting people to advocate for expanded insurance coverage, increased public understanding, quality treatment, and funding for research in their own states.[17] By signing up on the NEDA Web site, people get the latest advocacy updates for their own state by e-mail.

What Is the Worldwide Charter for Action on Eating Disorders?

The charter itself is a kind of patient's "bill of rights" for the treatment of eating disorders. The Academy developed it to encourage policy makers from around the world to commit to the actions it proposes. Below are the rights of people with eating disorders and caretakers as set forth by the charter.

I. Right to communication/partnership with health professionals

II. Right to comprehensive assessment and treatment planning

III. Right to accessible, high quality, fully-funded, specialized care

IV. Right to respectful, fully-informed, age-appropriate, safe levels of care

V. Right of carers to be informed, valued, and respected as a treatment resource

VI. Right of carers to accessible, appropriate support and education resources.[18]

ADVANCES IN DIAGNOSIS AND TREATMENT

More studies have been done on cognitive behavioral therapy (CBT) than on any other kind of therapy. The studies suggest that CBT is the most effective treatment, especially for bulimia. But it is not perfect. Family-based therapy (FBT) is the most successful in treating teens for anorexia. Newer treatments like dialectical behavior therapy and interpersonal therapy are proving to be effective, but need to be studied more. Meanwhile, the current criteria for diagnosing eating disorders are causing a lot of problems for patients and experts alike.

The DSM Problem

Many health experts believe that the criteria listed in the *DSM-IV-TR* for diagnosing anorexia, bulimia, and EDNOS are confusing, complicated, and must be changed. Insurance companies use these criteria to measure the severity of a patient's eating disorder. When patients with serious eating disorders do not fit the mold for anorexia or bulimia exactly, their insurance companies may not approve them for the care they need. More research is necessary before the current criteria for diagnosis can be changed.

Family-Based Therapies

Recently, family-based therapies have proven to be more effective than individual therapy in treating teens with anorexia and bulimia. The Maudsley Approach seems to be especially promising.

The Maudsley Approach is a family-based therapy for teens who have had anorexia for three years or less. Parents play an active role with the guidance of health professionals. There are three phases. In the first phase, parents are taught how to use their creativity in a positive way to give their child the foods she needs to restore health. When their child shows a steady weight gain, the second phase begins. Now parents help their child take more control over her eating. In the third phase, after the child has reached 95 percent of her ideal weight, the emphasis shifts to her establishing a healthy adolescent identity.

This approach is not for everyone. Parents are required to put in a lot of time and effort. But many of them think it is worth it. Research shows that 75 to 90 percent of patients still

Text Messaging a Therapist

There is one way to talk to a therapist without feeling embarrassed. Send a text message. One nurse-therapist tried it with her eating disorder patients. They were allowed to text her any time, Monday through Friday, between 8 A.M. and 6 P.M. They could also text in the evening and on weekends, but they would not get a response unless it was an emergency.

Text messaging is one way to contact a therapist without feeling embarrassed.

The nurse found that texting helped in a lot of ways. It gave her patients a chance to express their feelings right after something important happened, instead of waiting for the next appointment. Her patients were also comforted to know she was always there for them. It also gave the nurse time to think before she responded. Later, she could explore some of the text messages during therapy.

Continued on next page

Continued from previous page

The ability of her patients to express themselves varied, but the messages often reflected their type of eating disorder. Patients with anorexia, who tend to be perfectionists, usually sent well-organized messages with few spelling or grammar mistakes. Messages from bulimic patients were usually longer, disorganized, and emotional.

Texting seemed to improve the relationship between the nurse and her patients. It also helped ease some of her patients' feelings of shame and allowed them to be more engaged when working through issues.[20]

Who knows? Texting your therapist may be the wave of the future.

maintain their weight after five years.[19] That is a big improvement over the 50 percent recovery rate with other therapies.

The Maudsley Approach is also cost-effective. Most of the therapy takes place at home. The average teen with anorexia requires only fifteen to twenty outpatient treatment sessions over a six- to twelve-month period.

The same approach is being tested on teens with bulimia. The National Institute of Mental Health (NIMH) has financed a grant that studies these teens in the same family-based intervention, comparing them to those in two other individual therapies. Researchers will examine how effective each therapy is at reducing bingeing and purging episodes. They also want to learn what kind of effect the severity of symptoms will have on the teens' response to treatment.[21] Meanwhile, new research at the University of Connecticut is examining how family-based therapy can be developed for young adults.

The Internet and Eating Disorders

The Internet is a great place to find out about eating disorders. People can look up tools for self-assessment and information about treatment options. Therapy Web sites also exist, and they do have a few advantages: These cost less than conventional therapy, can be used anonymously, and are convenient for patients who do not have transportation or who live at a distance from an actual facility. Some professionals believe a therapy Web site can be used as an early intervention resource, but most agree that face-to-face therapy is a wiser choice.

One current study is exploring the possibility that an Internet, therapist-guided, chat support group for parents can be helpful with family-based treatment.[22] Internet support groups for people with eating disorders are not new. But experts warn that unregulated chat rooms can be dangerous. Unfortunately, there are some people on the Internet who are waiting to exploit anyone looking for support. So far, there has not been sufficient research done on how the Internet may help or harm patients with eating disorders.

Some professionals believe a therapy Web site can be used as an early intervention resource, but most agree that face-to-face therapy is a wiser choice.

ADVANCES IN RESEARCH

Researchers are still not certain about the nature of eating disorders and what causes them. The latest research suggests that eating disorders may be associated with abnormal brain activity. If mental disorders are actually brain disorders, how do they work? Finding the answers will require more research in the fields of genetics, neuroscience, and psychology.

fact OR fiction

Female Athletes Do Not Get Eating Disorders

Female athletes are too healthy to get eating disorders, right? Wrong. Believe it or not, all athletes have a greater risk for eating disorders, especially gymnasts, figure skaters, swimmers, and dancers.

These athletes have to be thin to succeed. At least, that is the accepted belief in the sports world. They often wear form-fitting clothes, which may make them feel self-conscious about their bodies. They also are used to being judged. Since the "best" athletes tend to be perfectionists, you have a recipe for anorexia.

Some athletes overcome these obstacles because they have supportive coaches who promote good health. Others have coaches who just want to win and will do what it takes to get there.

Female athletes are at an even greater risk for eating disorders than non-athletes.

Athletes with eating disorders are more likely to develop medical problems, because they already exercise strenuously and put pressure on their bodies. Female athletes even have their own disease called female athlete triad. This disorder affects eating habits, menstrual periods, and bone strength.

Being a dancer, gymnast, ice skater, or swimmer is great as long as people remember to be themselves first.

Genetics

Since the human genome sequence was published in 2003, researchers have been trying to locate the genes that are associated with a risk for developing an eating disorder. Chapter 4 discusses how the genes for anorexia may have been discovered on chromosome 1. Genes showing a susceptibility to bulimia nervosa have been found on chromosomes 10p and 14.[23]

Does that mean that genes cause eating disorders? Not exactly. Health experts believe it works like this: A person has a combination of genes that make her susceptible to an eating disorder. That means she may be influenced by the risk factors in her environment more easily. Those risk factors can be the media, dieting, trauma—all the ones mentioned in Chapter 4. Researchers like to call these risk factors "triggers" because they do just that—trigger eating disorders. For example, if a young woman has a weak genetic susceptibility, she may need a strong trigger to develop a disorder. If she has a strong susceptibility, a weak trigger may set her off. That is why studying other risk factors, along with genes, is so important.

Two grants in this area have been funded by NIMH. One will take a look at how psychological and biological factors affect food intake and feeling full for women with bulimia and purging disorder. The other will examine how the ovarian hormones estrogen and progesterone contribute to bulimic behavior. Researchers will also study which genes can affect these hormones.[24]

As future research explains more about how genes contribute to eating disorders, it may improve the ability to identify people who are at risk. Perhaps someday gene therapy will even be able to eliminate that risk.

Neuroimaging

Neuroimaging is a technique now being used to help understand eating disorders better. These tests allow doctors to examine the brain without actually penetrating the skin. Brain scans or MRIs (magnetic resonance imaging) are already used to identify abnormal brain activity in people with depression and obsessive-compulsive disorder (OCD). Now they are being used on people with eating disorders.

In one study, researchers examined the effects of impulsive behavior on the brain activity of women with bulimia, as compared to a control group who did not have bulimia. They focused on the part of the brain associated with self-control. Twenty women in each group were given a task that involved conflicting information. The bulimic women were more impulsive and made more mistakes when

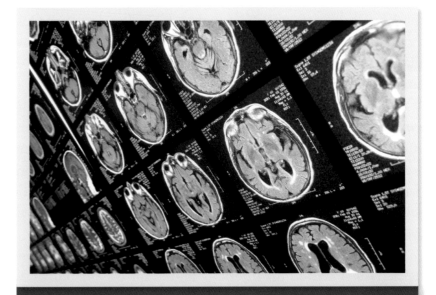

Advances in neuroimaging are helping researchers to better understand eating disorders.

compared to the control group. The patterns of brain activity were also different. The healthy women showed more brain activity. The women who were bulimic had less. The study indicated that women who are bulimic may have impaired brain activity.[25]

Another study using positron emission tomography (PET) scanning showed that women may not be able to control their hunger as well as men for biological reasons. The first day, both men and women were enticed with their favorite foods but were not allowed to eat. The next day, they were told to try not to want the food before they were enticed. The brain regions scanned were the ones associated with emotional regulation, conditioning, and the motivation to eat. Men showed less brain activity on the day they were asked to inhibit. Women showed no real difference. The study may help explain why women have more eating disorders than men, and why they usually have more trouble losing weight.[26]

A study using positron emission tomography (PET) scanning showed that women may not be able to control their hunger as well as men for biological reasons.

Other Areas of Research

Current studies run the gamut of eating disorder issues, from the media's influence on body image, to the danger of ending treatment prematurely, to using yoga as an addition

Be a Media Watchdog

Media Watchdogs are volunteers from all over the country who help monitor the media for programs or advertisements that impact body image—positively or negatively. When a notice is submitted to the NEDA, they look it over and decide how best to handle it.

The NEDA Web site provides a list of things to look for, like a picture of people eating a balanced meal (positive) or a computer-enhanced photo of an emaciated model (not so positive). Then they may ask the person who submitted the notice to answer a few simple questions. This program really works. Since it began in 1997, more than half of the advertisements that NEDA has protested were discontinued! You have the power to make a difference. Go to the NEDA Web site, click on "Programs & Events" and "Media Watchdog" to find out how.[27]

to therapy. New studies are making up for the lack of information about psychological factors in eating disorders. Researchers are also concentrating on the basic processes of eating disorders, to determine how they create risk factors. This information may help prevent eating disorders in the early stages.

Meanwhile, researchers need to learn more about the effects of brain chemistry on eating disorders so that better medications can be found. Studies must also continue among populations where little has been done so far—men, children, older people, and groups from diverse ethnic and racial backgrounds. Finally, people need to discover effective ways to counter the destructive influence of the media on body image in our culture.

In 2007, researcher and psychologist Cynthia Bulik summed it up when she said: "Understanding how genes and environment interact, both to increase risk for eating disorders and to protect those who are genetically vulnerable from developing the disorder, will require the cooperation of professionals in the eating disorders field, the media, and the fashion and entertainment industries. Only cooperatively, will we be able to move the field forward toward the elimination of this disease."[28]

CHAPTER SEVEN

Living With Eating Disorders

Wouldn't it be wonderful if recovering from an eating disorder was like recovering from the flu? A few days of rest, push the fluids, take some medicine, and you're back on your feet again. Unfortunately, eating disorders are some of the hardest illnesses to get over. The usual recovery time is two to seven years. Of course, treatment for eating disorders is worthwhile. Many people can and do recover and lead healthy, fulfilling lives.

It takes time to recover because the behaviors that go along with eating disorders become so deep-rooted that patients cannot get better without long-term therapy. Patients need to understand their behaviors—and then find effective ways to cope with their disorder. The longer a patient has an eating disorder, the harder it is to treat and the longer it takes to recover.

Treatment is the best hope for people with eating disorders. But recovery is not 100 percent guaranteed. Of those who get treatment, about half make a complete recovery and another 25 percent get considerably better. Sadly, 25 percent never get better even with treatment; some even die. But people rarely recover by themselves. Twenty percent of people who never go for treatment die.[1]

Intensive treatment in an inpatient facility or outpatient clinic lasts several months. Afterward, inpatients are discharged. Once home, all patients continue seeing a therapist, although not as often. Some patients may choose to have therapy for the rest of their lives, but others will taper off visits until, eventually, they only see a therapist a few times a year or not at all.

With the support of family and close friends, patients with eating disorders can return to a normal life.

The transition from inpatient treatment to home can be traumatic. And for both inpatients and outpatients, seeing their therapist less often is stressful. Relapses are common, especially in the beginning, and many people return to intensive treatment more than once. Learning to cope with everyday conflicts in a healthy way—not by slipping back into eating disorder behaviors—is a challenge. These skills are not learned overnight, which is why full recovery can take years.

WHAT IS RECOVERY?

Patients often ask their therapists, "When will I be well?" and "How will I know?" There is no concrete answer to these questions. For someone with anorexia, recovery involves reaching a healthy weight and, for females, starting to menstruate again. For a person with bulimia, it includes not bingeing or purging. In binge-eating syndrome, it means not eating uncontrollably. For all people with eating disorders, recovery means realizing that their self-worth does not depend on their weight or shape.

But these accomplishments are only part of what recovery is all about. The problems that led to the eating disorder have to be resolved, too. To paraphrase Ron Saxen, profiled in this chapter's "How Real People Deal," a person with an eating disorder can look great on the outside, but he is still the same "screwed-up" person inside.

cool ideas

The Empty Bowl

At dinnertime, set an extra place at the table and put an empty bowl there. Before eating, think about all the people close to home and around the world who do not have enough money for food and whose bowls are empty every day.

Filling an empty bowl to help those who can't afford food makes mealtimes more meaningful. It can help a person with eating disorders think about others in need instead of their own food issues.

Put some change in the empty bowl every day, whatever the household can afford. When the bowl is full, give the money to a local or national organization whose goal is to stop hunger. Give to a local food pantry or soup kitchen. Or go online and find national organizations that help fight world hunger.

The empty bowl idea was created by Heifer International. This organization donates farm animals to needy people around the world so they can become self-sufficient. Many churches, schools, and other organizations hold empty bowl fundraisers. But individuals and families can also help end world hunger—and give thanks for the food they have—by putting a few coins a day into their own empty bowls.

Trying to answer the question "What is recovery?", researchers at the University of Missouri surveyed ninety girls and women who had once had eating disorders. They asked what recovery meant to them. Here are some of their responses:

- Not being obsessed with food, calories, or exercise
- Having other things on their mind besides food
- No longer fearing food or feeling like they had to control their eating
- Not feeling bad or guilty about what they eat
- Being able to eat at a restaurant
- Not bingeing or purging
- Being able to eat in front of other people
- Being able to focus on life[2]

The study concluded that things that were absent (like bingeing and purging) and things that were present (like being able to eat out) both constituted recovery. Or to paraphrase Dr. James Lock, author of *Help Your Teenager Beat an Eating Disorder*, "Recovery may be when life replaces the eating disorder."[3]

EVERYDAY CHALLENGES

Unfortunately, life does not replace the eating disorder overnight. Discussing coping strategies with a therapist is one thing. Putting those strategies into real-life practice is something else entirely.

Obviously, anything related to food is stressful for someone in recovery. Imagine if a recovering alcoholic still had to drink three times a day. People recovering from eating disorders have to face—and eat—food at breakfast, lunch, and dinner. Exercising can also be stressful for someone who once used it as a purging behavior. But regular exercise is also vital to good health.

Some inpatient treatment facilities teach patients how to live with food in the real world. They teach them how to buy and cook food, not just how to eat healthfully. Patients who do not get this kind of instruction sometimes go back to their old habits once they are faced with shopping, preparing, and eating food on their own. Depending on the eating disorder, these everyday tasks can trigger a binge or make a patient stop eating again.

Some inpatient treatment facilities teach patients how to live with food in the real world. They teach them how to buy and cook food, not just how to eat healthfully.

While regular exercise is vital to good health, it can be stressful for someone who once used it as a purging behavior.

"Trigger" is a word often used when discussing eating disorders. It means the things that caused the eating disorder in the first place, such as dieting or a life-altering event, like going away to college. But a trigger can also be something that prompts a person with an eating disorder to binge, vomit, over-exercise, or restrict food even more. Triggers are everywhere, and people in recovery must learn to cope with them or they can relapse.

Anything that causes stress is a trigger. The stress of having to lose another five pounds when he was already starving was the trigger that drove model Ron Saxen back to binge eating.

Food itself is also a common trigger. Pizza, donuts, and other "forbidden" foods are the most common trigger foods. Sometimes just reading about these foods can cause a relapse.

Internet message boards and Web sites can also be potent triggers, even if the sites are meant to discourage eating disorders. Seeing photos of emaciated people or reading true accounts of eating disorders can cause people to revert to old eating disorder behaviors. Many of these sites actually warn: "Trigger alert: Do not read if you are recovering."

"Trigger" is a word often used when discussing eating disorders. It means the things that caused the eating disorder in the first place, such as dieting or a life-altering event, like going away to college.

Other triggers include problems at work, a big exam, breaking up with a boyfriend or girlfriend, marital problems, the death of a close friend or family member, problems getting along with parents, fear of recovery, and being around other people who have eating disorders.

Talking to a therapist about abuse, rape, or other traumatic events can also trigger a relapse. But these events are probably at the root of the eating disorder and must be discussed before the patient can get well. Patients need to warn their therapists that such issues are triggering so the therapist can deal with them appropriately.

HOW REAL PEOPLE DEAL: EATING HIS WAY OUT OF A JOB

A t age twenty-one, Ron Saxen had a promising career as a fashion model. He stood 6 feet 3 inches tall, weighed a muscular 179 pounds, and had cheekbones to die for. But he still felt like an impostor.

Ron was hiding a terrible secret. He had binge-eating disorder.

It started in childhood. He grew up in a very religious family with overly strict, abusive parents. Some nights, his father would come home late from work and wake up Ron and his four siblings and beat them. Ron felt so scared that he would lie in bed and sweat.

One night, he remembered there was a stash of candy in his closet for the school candy sale. He grabbed a bar and scoffed it down. "And when I ate it, it felt good," Ron remembered. "I forgot about what was about to happen, and then I went back and did it again, and again, and again."[4]

As he got older, he continued to use food to numb his feelings and fears. "I'd pull up to a McDonalds and get a couple of Big Macs, large fries, cheeseburger, and a chocolate shake," Ron said.[5] Then he'd head to Taco Bell for more food and follow that up with several candy bars and maybe another burger. Some days, he ate up to 15,000 calories—at least five times the amount an active teenage boy needs.

He felt ashamed, but he could not stop. Eventually, he ballooned to 280 pounds.

Over the years, Ron tried dieting. Sometimes he lost thirty or forty pounds, but he always gained it back. Once, he got down to 205 pounds, and people started asking if he was a model. He thought they were joking at first. When he realized they were serious, he got serious, too. He embarked on an intensive diet and exercise regimen, eating less than 1,000 calories a day and exercising to exhaustion. He would swim twenty-five laps, lift weights, bike thirty miles, and run five miles—all in one day!

In a few months, Ron was down to a trim 179 pounds. When a modeling agency hired him, he thought his life was finally perfect.

But Ron could not live with the constant pressure of staying thin that modeling requires. He was hungry, exhausted, and stressed out. He looked great, but admitted, "I was still the same screwed up guy."[6]

After Ron had been modeling for six months, he was asked to lose five pounds for an underwear fashion show. Something inside him snapped and he went on a food binge. He continued bingeing and refused to answer his agent's calls. Six months later, he had gained sixty pounds. His modeling career was over.

Ron spent more than twenty years binge eating before he finally sought help. He began reading books about eating disorders, and with the encouragement of friends, he started therapy and stopped bingeing. Today, Ron is forty-four years old, happily married, and the author of *The Good Eater*, a book about his life as a binge eater. He is a healthy weight, exercises normally, and has learned to eat when he is hungry and stop when he is full.

"It's important to recognize that any form of eating disorder is about emotional issues, it's about self-esteem issues that need to be addressed," he said. "It's not about size and it's not about food."[7]

Support Groups Are As Good As Therapy

Support groups are not as helpful to patients as therapy, but they can be helpful along with therapy. Support groups are appealing because they are usually free and people can drop in without making an appointment. Discussions are run by leaders called facilitators, and guest speakers often come to share their stories. But the major appeal of support groups is the chance to connect with other people who have eating disorders.

During their first few meetings, people should observe what is going on to be sure the group will be helpful and not harmful. Does the facilitator encourage people to get professional help? Are most of the people in the group in treatment? Is a healthy body image promoted? Are problem-solving ideas offered? If this is the case, the group will probably be helpful. But get out fast if they start exchanging ideas on how to diet or purge. And remember: These groups are not a substitute for one-on-one therapy with a professional.

HEADING OFF A RELAPSE

How can people prevent a relapse? One way is by being prepared. People in recovery need to make a list of things that have triggered bingeing, purging, or other behaviors in the past and plan healthy ways of coping. Planning ahead also works when a stressful event is scheduled for the future.

Another way to prevent a relapse is to know the warning signs. When someone starts to think and act like they did before treatment, they may be ready to relapse. For example, thinking about food and calories a lot, looking in the mirror or stepping on the scale often, feeling guilty after eating, or

What Is a Relapse?

A relapse is the reappearance of symptoms of a disease after the patient has been well for a while. Relapses are common in eating disorders, occurring in about one-third of all patients.[8] They can occur at any time, including right after coming home from inpatient treatment. Some patients recover and relapse several times before they get well.

Studies show that patients who continue therapy are less apt to relapse. Although regular sessions are best, any kind of therapeutic communication helps. In 2003, German researchers studied a group of bulimic patients who had just been discharged from an inpatient facility. Once a week for six months, the patients sent text messages to therapists, who replied with a mixture of programmed and personal information. The study concluded that text messaging is an effective way of supporting bulimic patients.[9]

feeling depressed and hopeless are all signs a relapse is on the horizon.

A person who slips back into eating disorder behaviors should not feel ashamed, guilty, or like a failure. The therapist will help the patient determine what triggered the relapse so together they can plan how to avoid another one.

COPING STRATEGIES

Eating disorder triggers usually cannot be avoided, so people must learn to deal with them. Therapists and nutritionists will help patients come up with coping strategies. There are also

A number of coping strategies, such as scheduling time for a favorite hobby, can help prevent relapse into an eating disorder.

lots of useful tips on Web sites devoted to eating disorders recovery. These tips help people stay motivated and offer alternatives to unhealthy behaviors. Here is a sampling of the advice offered:

Motivational Exercises

- Keep a journal of things to be thankful for and write in it every night, listing even small things.
- Put sticky notes around the house with positive messages, such as, "I am lovable just the way I am" or "I can find inner peace."

- Stay more aware of your surroundings by changing your daily routine. Take a different route to school or work, go to a new mall or grocery store, or just put clothes on in a different order.
- Carry or wear a special object to help feel in control when faced with a stressful situation. For example, feel a smooth stone or wear a piece of jewelry from someone special.
- Release anger by writing a "Dear Eating Disorder" letter. Tell the disorder what you hate about it, list all the things it kept you from accomplishing in life, and say how it has made you sick and why you want it gone forever. Then destroy the letter in a symbolic fashion, such as burning it in the fireplace or putting it through a paper shredder.
- Schedule time for yourself. For example, take a walk, read a book, or go to a movie. Start with two hours a week and increase the time.
- Celebrate "Happy Recovery Day" by buying yourself inexpensive gifts. Wrap them and present one to yourself every time you make a small step in the recovery process, like exercising for only an hour or not purging for a few days.
- Make a list of trusted people you can turn to for support, along with their phone numbers and email addresses. Leave one copy at home and carry the other with you.[10]

Alternatives to Eating Disorder Behaviors

Healthy behaviors provide alternatives to starving, bingeing, purging, or over-exercising. People should keep a list of alternative behaviors and try different ones to see which work the best. Items on the list should be easy, fun, relaxing, or just plain silly.

Here are some ideas: Take a walk, take a nap, read a book, listen to music and dance, take a bubble bath, play with your dog, doodle on paper, color in a coloring book, go for a long

It's important to identify alterntives to eating disorder behaviors, like taking a walk.

drive, hug someone, pop bubble wrap, call a friend, go to a movie by yourself, clean your closet and donate old clothes to charity, take all your loose change to a coin machine, take a deep breath and count to ten, call a hotline, call your therapist.[11]

Other Helpful Advice

No matter what their eating disorder, people should make sure to keep all therapy sessions, follow their meal plans if they have them, take any vitamins the doctor has prescribed, surround themselves with supportive people, and exercise moderately (no more than an hour a day).

People with anorexia and bulimia should not diet, avoid frequently weighing themselves or looking in the mirror, remember what a healthy weight is for their bodies, not skip meals, and find positive role models—not ultra-thin celebrities.[12, 13]

People with binge-eating syndrome also should not diet, even if they are overweight. Dieting can trigger a binge-eating episode. They should eat breakfast because it makes them less likely to eat too much later in the day. They should not stockpile food because this increases the temptation to binge. They should check with their doctors about what kind of exercise program is safe if they have health problems related to obesity. They should also try not to be too hard on themselves because of their weight.[15]

What Is Intuitive Eating?

A French proverb says, "A good meal ought to begin with hunger." That is the philosophy behind intuitive eating. It means listening to and obeying the body's cues about hunger and fullness. Many people, and not just those with eating disorders, eat when they are bored, nervous, lonely, or tired. Pretty soon, they forget to listen to their body's hunger signals.

People also overeat so often, they do not realize when they are full. The body does not register fullness until about twenty minutes after eating.[14] So eating too fast can lead to second helpings and overeating. Eating deserves people's full attention. They should sit, not stand, turn off the TV, put down the newspaper, and enjoy the smell, taste, and texture of their food.

People who eat when they are hungry and stop when they are full do not have weight problems. Intuitive eating is something everyone should strive for, not just people recovering from eating disorders.

FAMILY CHALLENGES

When a family member has an eating disorder, the entire household is disrupted. Instead of being a chance to relax and socialize, mealtimes are stressful occasions for everyone, not just the person with the eating disorder. Going to a restaurant, having a holiday dinner, or going on vacation are difficult. Treatment can be a huge financial drain on the family, especially if insurance does not cover the costs. When the person with the eating disorder is a husband or wife, the spouse can feel angry, helpless, and hurt, believing the person prefers the eating disorder to them. These issues can tear families apart.

Family therapy is vitally important in helping people sort out these problems. The therapist will discuss several ways to make the patient's recovery easier for everyone. Some do's and don'ts for families are listed below.

Eating disorders are difficult for the whole family.

Don't expect a quick fix: People with eating disorders can take years to fully recover. Learn to be satisfied with small steps toward health.

Don't get into power struggles: Do not make mealtimes a battleground by trying to control the person's eating or by offering bribes or rewards. Let the professionals handle this. Some control may be necessary in families with adolescents, where treatments like the Maudsley Approach have been successful (see Chapter 6).

Don't look for causes or assign blame: This only makes the person with the eating disorder feel more guilty and ashamed. Causes are best explored in family therapy.

Don't ask how you can help: Ask the therapist for advice, not the person with the eating disorder.

Don't answer questions about weight: Never answer "yes" or "no" when asked "Do I look fat in this?" Instead, say something like, "It's best if we avoid talking about your weight."

Don't prepare special meals: Buying favorite foods is fine, but do not bend over backward. People with eating disorders have to learn to eat what everyone else eats.

Don't become a watchdog: Even if the person asks, do not monitor how much they eat or whether they purge. They need to take responsibility for their own health.

Do be affectionate: Give the person hugs, plan special activities together, and leave encouraging notes around the house.

Do realize your limitations: Learn to say no and set rules. For example, no laxatives or diet pills are allowed in the house. Other reasonable rules are expecting the person to clean the bathroom if she purges and to pay for the food she ate during a binge.

Take care of yourself: Talk to friends, join a support group, or see your own therapist.[16]

LIVING WITH PERMANENT PROBLEMS

Sadly, some people with eating disorders end up with lifelong physical problems. Teens that restrict food when a growth spurt normally occurs can disrupt the secretion of growth hormone so they stay short for life. People who abuse laxatives can have such severe constipation they need surgery to have their large intestine removed. Other permanent complications include osteoporosis and severe dental problems, which are discussed in earlier chapters.

Sadly, some people with eating disorders end up with lifelong physical problems.

In women, infertility (the inability to become pregnant) may be a permanent complication of anorexia. Some females with anorexia stop menstruating and never start again, or they have irregular menstrual cycles. About one in five women who visit infertility clinics once had an eating disorder.[17]

The good news is that about 75 percent of women who recover from eating disorders are able to get pregnant.[18] But a study published in 2007 shows that pregnancy can actually trigger binge-eating disorder. The University of North Carolina and the University of Oslo, Norway, studied 41,000 pregnant women, including some with eating disorders. Thirty-nine percent of those with binge-eating disorder stopped bingeing during pregnancy, but binge eating was the only disorder that showed a significant number of new cases (711) occurring during pregnancy. Women who had never had the disorder developed it during pregnancy.[19]

Most women who have recovered from eating disorders have healthy pregnancies, including those who had anorexia. However, some studies suggest these women might have more difficult deliveries, cesarean sections, miscarriages, and babies born prematurely or with low birth weights. Postpartum depression may also be more common. Women who are overweight from binge-eating disorder may develop temporary diabetes during pregnancy and have overweight babies.

The ideal time to become pregnant is after a woman has recovered fully from an eating disorder. But this does not always happen. Women who are still recovering physically and emotionally when they get pregnant must be totally honest with their doctors about their medical history. The doctor may want to monitor the baby's development and the mother's health even more closely than usual.

* * *

Why do people starve, binge, and purge until their lives are consumed and their health is ruined? Researchers are still trying to solve this mystery. Every day, we learn more and more about eating disorders. But many more studies must be done before these complex illnesses are fully understood. When they are, millions of people will learn to enjoy life, and food, again.

Eating Disorders Timeline

500–323 B.C.: Reports from classical Greece describe people overeating.

430 B.C.: Herodotus writes that Egyptians purge for three days every month for health reasons.

323–146 B.C.: Male hermits in Greece renounce the material world by starving themselves.

4 B.C.–65 A.D.: Seneca writes that the Romans "eat to vomit and vomit to eat."

383 A.D.: First anorexia death is recorded.

1200–1600: There are 181 reports of women starving themselves for religious reasons.

1380: St. Catherine of Siena, Italy, dies from self-starvation at the age of thirty-three.

1689: Dr. Richard Morton publishes *A Treatise of Consumption*, the first written medical account of anorexia.

1831–1901: Victorian Era sees a surge in anorexia cases among middle- and upper-class girls.

1862: French physician Louis Victor Marcé identifies anorexia as a psychiatric disorder.

1873: Dr. Charles Lesègue of France publishes *On Hysterical Anorexia*, describing the disease's medical symptoms; Dr. William Gull, physician to Queen Victoria, coins the term *anorexia nervosa*.

1973: Hilde Bruch publishes *Eating Disorders*, arguing that self-starvation is a struggle for control and self-respect.

1979: British psychiatrist Gerald Russell describes bulimia as a variation of anorexia nervosa and names it *bulimia nervosa*.

1980: The third edition of the *Diagnostic and Statistical Manual (DSM-III)* of the American Psychiatric Association classifies anorexia nervosa as a mental disorder.

1983: Popular singer/musician Karen Carpenter dies from heart failure due to anorexia, bringing the crisis of eating disorders to the attention of the media and general public.

1987: The revised edition of the *Diagnostic and Statistical Manual (DSM-III-R)* of the American Psychiatric Association classifies bulimia nervosa as a mental disorder.

1993: The Academy for Eating Disorders, an organization of eating disorders professionals from the education, treatment, and research fields, holds its first meeting.

1994: Binge-eating disorder is recognized as an Eating Disorder Not Otherwise Specified (EDNOS), but it is not yet classified as a distinct mental disorder.

2002: Researchers at the University of Pittsburgh discover possible genetic links to anorexia on chromosome 1.

2008: Congress passes the Mental Health Parity Law requiring insurance companies to give mental illness equal status with physical illness in its coverage.

Chapter Notes

Chapter 1: Straight Talk About Eating Disorders

1. CNN.com, "Showbiz Tonight: Hollywood's Obsession with Weight," December 29, 2005, <http://transcripts.cnn.com/TRANSCRIPTS/0512/29/sbt.01.html> (February 11, 2009).

2. CNN.com, "'Sopranos' Star's Struggle with Eating Disorder," November 7, 2005, <http://www.cnn.com/2005/HEALTH/conditions/11/02/discala.eating/disorder/index.html> (February 11, 2009).

3. CNN.com, "Showbiz Tonight: Hollywood's Obsession with Weight."

4. Ibid.

5. CBS News, "'Sopranos' Star Tells of Anorexia Battle," August 19, 2002, <http://www.cbsnews.com/stories/2002/08/19/earlyshow/leisure/books/printables519147.shtml> (February 11, 2009).

6. Kristin Dizon, "A Moment with . . . Jamie-Lynn Sigler, Actress/Singer/Eating Disorders Spokeswoman," *Seattle Post-Intelligencer*, February 26, 2003.

7. Jamie Lynn Sigler, *Wise Girl: What I've Learned About Life, Love, and Loss* (New York: Pocket Books, 2002).

8. Ibid.

9. CNN.com, "Showbiz Tonight: Hollywood's Obsession with Weight."

10. Centers for Disease Control and Prevention, "Defining Overweight and Obesity," <http://www.cdc.gov/nccdphp/dnpa/obesity/defining.htm> (February 22, 2009).

11. National Institute of Mental Health, "Study Tracks Prevalence of Eating Disorders," February 9, 2007, <http://www.nimh.gov/science-news/2007/study-tracks-prevalance-of-eating-disorders.shtml> (February 12, 2009).

12. Carolyn Costin, *The Eating Disorder Sourcebook*, 3rd ed. (New York: McGraw Hill, 2007), pp. 123–124.

13. James I. Hudson, et al., "The Prevalence and Correlates of Eating Disorders in the National Comorbidity Survey Replication," *Biological Psychiatry*, Vol. 61, No. 3, February, 2007, pp. 348–358.

14. Costin, p. 37.

15. Johns Hopkins Health Alerts, "Eating Disorders: Not Just for the Young," <http://www.johnshopkinshealthalerts.com/reports/depression_anxiety/2194-1.html?type=pf> (February 12, 2009).

16. Web4Health, "Eating Disorders Statistics," August 8, 2008, <http://web4health.info/en/answers/ed-other-incidence.htm> (February 10, 2009).

17. Costin, p. 24.

18. National Eating Disorders Association, "In the News," <http://www.nationaleatingdisorders.org/in-the-news> (February 15, 2009).

19. The Renfrew Center Foundation for Eating Disorders, "Eating Disorders 101 Guide: A Summary of Issues, Statistics and Resources," revised October 2003, <http://www.renfrew.org> (February 15, 2009).

20. Kathleen N. Franco, "Eating Disorders," The Cleveland Clinic Center for Continuing Education, <http://www.clevelandclinicmeded.com/medicalpubs/diseasemanagement/psychiatry/eating> (February 13, 2009).

21. National Institute of Mental Health, "Eating Disorders," <http://www.nimh.nih.gov/health/topics/eating-disorders/index.shtml> (February 13, 2009).

22. Amy Scholten, "Risk Factors for Eating Disorders," Aurora Health Care, <http://www.aurorahealthcare.org/yourhealtah/healthgate/getcxontent.asp?URLhealthgate=%2220315.html%22> (February 10, 2009).

23. The Renfrew Center Foundation for Eating Disorders, "Eating Disorders 101 Guide: A Summary of Issues, Statistics and Resources."

24. Costin, p. 31.

25. Caring Online, "Eating Disorders News: Celebrities," <http://caringonline.com/eatdis/celebrities_a.html> (February 17, 2009).

26. Geocities, "Celebrities with Eating Disorders," <http://www.geocities.com/edpetition/CeLebritIesWithEatDis.html?200917> (February 17, 2009).

27. Casa Palmera, "Top 20 Famous Athletes with Eating Disorders," <http://www.casapalmera.com/articles/well-known-stories-of-athletes-with-eating-disorders> (February 17, 2009).

Chapter 2: The Science of Eating Disorders

1. The Renfrew Center Foundation for Eating Disorders, "Eating Disorders 101 Guide: A Summary of Issues, Statistics and Resources," <http://www.renfrew.org> (February 20, 2009).

2. Jeannette Curtis, "Anorexia Nervosa," National Alliance on Mental Illness of New York City, Inc., <http://newyorkcity.ny.networkofcare.org/mh/library/hwdetail.cfm?hwid=hw46497&cat=search> (February 18, 2009).

3. American Psychiatric Association, "Let's Talk about Eating Disorders," <http://www.healthyminds.org/multimedia/eatingdisorders.pdf> (February 18, 2009).

4. National Eating Disorders Association, "Anorexia Nervosa," <http://nationaleatingdisorders.org/p.asp?WebPage_ID=286&Profile_ID=41142> (February 18, 2009).

5. Ibid.

6. LovetoKnow.com, "Average Height and Weight for Teenager," <http://teens.lovetoknow.com/Average_Height_and_Weight_for_ Teenager> (February 21, 2009).

7. "Bailey Had Weird Eating Rituals," adapted from "Are You a Freaky Eater?" *Seventeen*, August, 2008, pp. 159–161.

8. The Renfrew Center Foundation for Eating Disorders.

9. Be Well @ Stanford, "How many calories do I need a day?" <http://stanford.wellsphere.com/healthy-eating-article/how-many-calories-do-i-need-a-day/34051> (February 21, 2009).

10. Carolyn Costin, *The Eating Disorder Sourcebook*, 3rd ed. (New York: McGraw Hill, 2007), p. 12.

11. National Eating Disorders Association, "Statistics," <http://www.nationaleatingdisorders.org/information-resources/general-information.php> (February 22, 2009).

12. Costin, p. 25.

13. National Eating Disorders Association, "Bulimia Nervosa," <http://www.nationaleatingdisorders.org/p.asp?WebPage_ID=286&Profile_ID=41141> (February 18, 2009).

14. Costin, p. 13.

15. WebMD, "Binge Eating Disorder—Topic Overview," <http://www.webmd.com/mental-health/binge-eating-disorder/tc/binge-eating-disorder-topic-overview> (February 15, 2009).

16. National Eating Disorders Association, "Eating Concerns and Oral Health," <http://www.nationaleatingdisorder.org/nedaDir/files/documents/handouts/OralHealth.pdf> (February 22, 2009).

17. National Eating Disorders Association, "Binge Eating Disorder," <http://www.nationaleatingdisorders.org/p.asp?WebPage_ID=286&Profile_ID=41140> (February 22, 2009).

18. Costin, p. 18.

19. *Diagnostic and Statistical Manual of Mental Disorders, Vol. 4, Text Revision* <http://www.dsmivtr.org> (February 20, 2009).

20. R. Robert Auger, "Sleep-Related Eating Disorders," *Psychiatry 2006*, Vol. 3, No. 11, November, 2006, pp. 64–70.

21. Costin, p. 213.

22. Ibid.

23. Ibid.

Chapter 3: History of Eating Disorders

1. Richard Carpenter, "A Brother Remembers," *People*, Vol. 20, No. 21, 1983, <http://www.people.com/people/archive/article/0,20198418,00.html> (February 20, 2009).

2. Michael Quinian, "Vomitorium," World Wide Words, <http://www.worldwidewords.org/weirdwords/ww-vom1.htm> (April 14, 2009)

3. Lucius Annaeas Seneca and Moses Hadas (translator), *The Stoic Philosophy of Seneca* (New York: W. W. Norton & Co., 1968), p. 120, <http://books.google.com/books?id=e6pvK6SQuvgC&pg=PA120&lpg=PA120 &dq=Seneca++wrote+eat+to+vomit&source=bl&ots=_3S78fVpAy&sig= GbUfmsrMNbdgE3KkBxWaxjBFy6Y&hl=en&ei=zQKnSZXKBJO5twf WgcnjDw&sa=X&oi=book_result&resnum=10&ct=result#PPA120,M1> (February 20, 2009).

4. Jules R. Bemporad, MD, "The Prehistory of Anorexia Nervosa," *The Psychoanalytic Approach to Psychosomatics and Eating Disorders: The Newsletter of the Psychosomatic Discussion Group of the American Psychoanalytic Association*, n.d., <http://www.cyberpsych.org/pdg/ pdghist.htm> (February 20, 2009).

5. Ibid.

6. H. G. Morgan, "Girls and Our Attitudes to Them," *British Medical Journal*, Vol. 2 (6103), December 24, 1977, pp. 1652–1655, <http://www.pubmedcentral.nih.gov/articlerender.fcgi?artid=1633278> (February 20, 2009).

7. David M. Garner and Paul E. Garfinkel, *Handbook of Treatment for Eating Disorders: Second Edition* (New York: Guilford Press, 1997), p. 3, <http://books.google.com/books?id=3gmogQshI_MC&printsec= frontcover#PPA2,M1> (February 20, 2009).

8. Ibid., p. 4.

9. Ibid., pp. 4–5.

10. Ibid., pp. 4–5.

11. "A Fear of Food: A History of Eating Disorders," Random History, August 8, 2008, <http://www.randomhistory.com/2008/08/08_eating.html> (February 20, 2009).

12. Garner and Garfinkel, p. 7.

13. Carolyn Costin, *The Eating Disorder Sourcebook*, 3rd ed. (New York: McGraw Hill, 2007), p. 36.

14. Ibid., p. 7.

15. Dr. C. George Boeree, "Ludwig Binswanger," *Personality Theories*, 1997.

16. Merry N. Miller, MD, and A. Pumariega, MD, "Eating Disorders: Culture and Eating Disorders," Healthy Place, December 12, 2008, <http://www.healthyplace.com/eating-disorders/main/eating-disorders-culture-and-eating-disorders/menu-id-58/> (February 20, 2009).

17. National Eating Disorders Association, "Research Results on Eating Disorders in Diverse Populations," 2006, <http://www.nationaleating disorders.org/nedaDir/files/documents/handouts/RsrchPop.pdf> (February 20, 2009).

18. Kathy Bunch, "Culture Shock: Fitting In, Losing Out," MedicineNet.com, January 15, 2001 (reviewed January 30, 2005), <http://www.medicineet.com/script/main/art.asp?articlekey=51270> (February 20, 2009).

19. Staff writer, "Cultural Aspects of Eating Disorders," Healthy Place, December 27, 2008, <http://www.healthyplace.com/eating-disorders/main/cultural-aspects-of-eating-disorders/menu-id-58/> (February 20, 2009).

20. The Alliance for Eating Disorders Awareness, "Eating Disorders Statistics," n.d., <http://www.eatingdisorderinfo.org/Resources/EatingDisordersStatistics/tabid/964/Default.aspx> (February 20, 2009).

Chapter 4: Risk Factors and Preventing Eating Disorders

1. Eating Disorders Coalition, "Eating Disorder Statistics," n.d., <http://www.eatingdisorderscoalition.org/documents/Statistics_000.pdf> (February 27, 2009).

2. Nicholas Bakalar, "National Survey Finds Eating Disorders on the Rise," *International Herald Tribune*, February 6, 2007, <http://www.iht.com/articles/2007/02/06/healthscience/sneating.php> (February 27, 2009).

3. Ibid.

4. Margarita Tartakovsky, "Eating Disorders in Men," *PsychCentral*, October 7, 2008, <http://psychcentral.com/blog/archives/2008/10/07/eating-disorders-in-men/> (April 14, 2009).

5. "Frequently Asked Questions," Office on Women's Health, U.S. Department of Health and Human Services, <http://www.womenshealth.gov/faq/alpha-index.cfm> (February 27, 2009).

6. Karen R. Koenig, "'Normal Eating,' Eating Disorders Blog," August 23, 2007, <http://www.eatingdisordersblogs.com/healthy/2007/08/how-culture-aff.html> (February 27, 2009).

7. National Institute on Media and the Family, "Media's Effect on Girls: Body Image and Gender Identity," rev. September 6, 2002, <http://www.mediafamily.org/facts/facts_mediaeffect.shtml> (February 27, 2009).

8. Louise Story, "Anywhere the Eye Can See, It's Likely to See an Ad," *New York Times*, January 15, 2007, <http://www.nytimes.com/2007/01/15/business/media/15everywhere.html?ref=business> (February 27, 2009).

9. Jennifer L. Derenne, MD, and Eugene V. Beresia, MD, "Body Image, Media, and Eating Disorders," *Academic Psychiatry*, 30: 257–261, May/June 2006, <http://ap.psychiatryonline.org/cgi/content/full/30/3/257> (February 27, 2009).

10. National Institute on Media and the Family.

11. Jack Neff, "Skinny Women Better for Bottom Line," *Advertising Age*, July 30, 2008, <http://adage.com/results.php?&endeca=1&return=endeca&search_offset=0&search_order_by=score&search_phrase=07/30/2008&D=07%2F30%2F2008&Nty=1&N=4294967221> (February 27, 2009).

12. Anne E. Becker, et al., "Eating Behaviors and Attitudes following prolonged exposure to television among ethnic Fijian adolescent girls," *British Journal of Psychiatry*, 180: 509–514, 2002,

<http://bjp.rcpsych.org/cgi/content/full/180/6/509?maxtoshow=
&HITS=10&hits=10&RESULTFORMAT=&fulltext=Fiji&searchid=
1&FIRSTINDEX=0&resourcetype=HWCIT> (February 27, 2009).

13. National Eating Disorders Association, "Statistics: Eating Disorders and Their Precursors," 2008, <http://www.nationaleatingdisorders.org/ p.asp?WebPage_ID=286&Profile_ID=41138> (February 27, 2009).

14. Ibid.

15. Carolyn Costin, *The Eating Disorder Sourcebook*, 3rd ed. (New York: McGraw Hill, 2007), pp. 59–60.

16. "MyPyramid.gov: Steps to a Healthier Diet," United States Department of Agriculture, (updated February 20, 2009), <http://www.mypyramid.gov/> (February 27, 2009).

17. FitCommerce.com, "Prejudice Against Fat People Still Common—Tyra Banks Excluded," February 16, 2007, <http://www.fitcommerce.com/Blueprint/Preju-dice-Against-Fat-People-Still-Common----Tyra-Banks-Excluded_page.aspx? pageId=276&announcementId=1113&tabId=87&tabIndex=0&portalId=2&cid =112> (February 27, 2009).

18. Health24.com, "Prejudice against fat people on TV," n.d., <http://www.health24.com/dietnfood/Weight_Centre/15-51-89,14715.asp> (February 20, 2009).

19. Carolyn Newsome and Jim Schettler, "Family Dynamics in Eating Disorders: An Introduction," *The Remuda Review*, Vol. 3, No. 2, Spring, 2004, <http://www.remudaranch.com/review/family_dynamics_in_eating_disorders/ index.php> (February 20, 2009).

20. Ashley Williams, "I Was Anorexic," *People*, Vol. 69, No. 5, February 11, 2008, <http://www.people.com/people/archive/article/0,20175690,00.html> (February 27, 2008).

21. Ibid.

22. Caris Davis, "New Miss America Opens Up About Anorexia Battle," *People*, Vol. 69, No. 3, January 28, 2008, <http://www.people.com/people/article/0,20174118,00.html> (February 27, 2009).

23. Williams.

24. Davis.

25. Lauren Bishop, "Miss America Looks Back," *Cincinnati Enquirer*, January 22, 2009, <http://news.cincinnati.com/article/20090122/LIFE/ 901220307> (February 27, 2009).

26. The Associated Press, "Miss America helps people conquer eating disorders," BG Views, January 23, 2009, <http://www.bgviews.com/2.6190/ 1.1588778-1.1588778> (February 27, 2009).

27. Jess Haines et al., "Weight Teasing and Disordered Eating Behaviors in Adolescents: Longitudinal Findings From Project EAT (Eating Among Teens)," *Pediatrics*, Vol.117, No. 2, February 2006, <http://pediatrics. aappublications.org/cgi/content/full/117/2/e209> (February 20, 2009).

28. Costin, p. 32.

29. Craig Johnson and Cindy Bulik, "Brave New World: The Role of Genetics in the Prevention and Treatment of Eating Disorders," *A Collaborative Study of the Genetics of Anorexia Nervosa and Bulimia Nervosa*, The Department of Psychiatry, University of Pittsburgh School of Medicine, (modified February 12, 2008), <http://www.wpic.pitt.edu/research/pfanbn/genetics.html>.

30. Ibid.

31. D.E. Grice et al., "Evidence for a Susceptibility Gene for Anorexia Nervosa on Chromosome 1," *The American Journal of Human Genetics*, 2002, <http://www.sciencedirect.com/science?_ob=ArticleURL&_udi=B8JDD-4R16S7F-V&_user=10&_rdoc=1&_fmt=&_orig=search&_sort=d&view=c&_acct=C000050221&_version=1&_urlVersion=0&_userid=10&md5=c51acf2b0473a67e6ad802c896830c44> (February 20, 2009).

32. Tori DeAngelis, "A Genetic Link to Anorexia," *Monitor on Psychology*, Vol. 33, No. 3, March 2002, <http://www.apa.org/monitor/mar02/genetic.html> (February 20, 2009).

33. Walter H. Kaye, MD and Michael Strober, PhD, "Serotonin: Implications for the Etiology & Treatment of Eating Disorders," *Eating Disorders Review*, Vol. 10, No. 3, May/June 1999, <http://www.gurze.com/client/client_pages/newsletter22.cfm> (February 20, 2009).

34. Hsien Hsien Lei, "Genetics of Anorexia and Bulimia," *Blisstree*, September 12, 2005, <http://www.blisstree.com/geneticsandhealth/genetics-of-anorexia-and-bulimia/> (February 20, 2009).

35. "Diabulimia," Juvenile Diabetes Research Foundation International, July 26, 2007, <http://www.jdrf.org/index.cfm?fuseaction=home.viewPage&page_id=FDF69313-1279-CFD5-A79B429F10056B6F> (February 27, 2009).

36. "Diabetes and Eating Disorders," *dLife*, (reviewed by Francine Kaufman, MD, April 2008, modified January 27, 2009), <http://www.dlife.com/dLife/do/ShowContent/daily_living/kids/eating_disorders.html> (February 27, 2009).

37. "MyPyramid.gov: Steps to a Healthier Diet," United States Department of Agriculture, (updated February 20, 2009), <http://www.mypyramid.gov/> (February 27, 2009).

Chapter 5: Diagnosis and Treatment

1. Quotations Book, <http://quotationsbook.com/quote/41228/> (February 25, 2009).

2. Christine Lagorio, "Diet Plan Success Tough to Weigh," January 3, 2005, CBS News, <http://www.cbsnews.com> (February 24, 2009).

3. National Institute of Mental Health, "Eating Disorders," <http://www.nimh.nih.gov/healthpublications/eating-disorders/pdf> (February 25, 2009).

4. "Treatment of Binge-Eating Disorder," All about Binge Eating, <http://www.binge-eating.com/treatment-binge-eating-disorder.php> (February 24, 2009).

5. CNN.com, "Paula Zahn Now: Inspirational Stories," December 23, 2005, <http://transcripts.cnn.com/TRANSCRIPTS/0512/23/pzn.01.html> (March 2, 2009).

6. Ibid.

7. Ibid.

8. Carolyn Costin, *The Eating Disorder Sourcebook*, 3rd ed. (New York: McGraw Hill, 2007), p. 8.

9. "The SCOFF Eating Disorders Test," Fitness: MSNBC.com, <http://www.msnbc.msn.com/id/3296439/> (Feb. 26, 2009).

10. "Bulimia Overview: Treatment for Anorexia," *New York Times Health*, <http://health.nytimes.com/health/guides/disease/bulimia/treatment-for-anorexia.html> (March 1, 2008)

11. "Bone Mineral Density in Bulimic Women—Influence of Endocrine Factors and Previous Anorexia," *European Journal of Endrocrinology*, Vol. 155, No. 2, 2006, pp. 245–251.

12. Ibid.

13. "Binge-eating Disorder," MayoClinic.com, <www.mayoclinic.com/print/binge-eating-disorder/DS00608/DSECTION=tests-and-diagnosis#> (March 1, 2009).

14. "Treatment of Anorexia Nervosa," *APA Practice Guidelines: Treatment of Patients with Eating Disorders*, p. 1, <http://www.psychiataryonline.com/content.aspxaID=139844> (March 1, 2009).

15. Costin, p. 218.

16. "New Approach Successful for Most Eating Disorders," *Medline Plus*, December 22, 2008, <http://www.nlm.nih.gov/medlineplus/print/news/fullstory_73036.html> (February 24, 2009).

17. "Interpersonal Psychotherapy Found Effective for Eating Disorder," *Psychiatric News*, October 4, 2002, <http://pn.psychiatryonline.org/cgi/content/full/37/19/20> (March 1, 2009).

18. "Treatment of Binge-Eating Disorder," *APA Practice Guidelines: Treatment of Patients with Eating Disorders*, p. 12, <http://www.psychiataryonline.com/content.aspxaID=139844> (March 1, 2009).

19. Costin, p. 248.

Chapter 6: Outlook for the Future

1. Bettina E. Bernstein, D.O., "Eating Disorder: Anorexia," *emedicine*, (updated March 31, 2008), <http://emedicine.medscape.com/article/912187-overview> (March 5, 2009).

2. Margo Maine, "Securing Eating Disorders Treatment: Ammunition for Arguments with Third Parties," National Eating Disorders Association, 2004, <http://www.nationaleatingdisorders.org/nedaDir/files/documents/handouts/SecrTxAm.pdf> (March 5, 2009).

3. "Eating Disorder Statistics," EatingDisorder.com, n.d.,
   <http://www.eatingdisorder.com/eating-disorders-statistics.html>
   (March 5, 2009).

4. National Association of Anorexia Nervosa and Associated Eating Disorders,
   "Anad Fact Sheet," n.d., <http://www.anad.org/5148/525801.html>
   (March 5, 2009).

5. Eating Disorders Coalition for Research, Policy & Action on Facebook,
   <http://www.facebook.com/group.php?gid=2216595438> (March 5, 2009).

6. "Anad Fact Sheet."

7. "EDC Mission," Eating Disorders Coalition for Research, Policy & Action,
   2008, <http://www.eatingdisorderscoalition.org/mission.htm> (March 5, 2009).

8. "State Mental Health Parity Laws 2007," National Alliance on Mental Illness,
   (updated April 2007), <http://www.nami.org/Template.cfm?
   Section=Parity1&Template=/ContentManagement/ContentDisplay.
   cfm&ContentID=45313> (March 5, 2009).

9. "National Eating Disorders Association Announces Results of Eating
   Disorders Poll on College Campuses across the Nation," National Eating
   Disorders Association, September 26, 2006,
   <http://www.nationaleatingdisorders.org/nedaDir/files/documents/PressRoom/
   CollegePoll_9-28-06.doc> (March 5, 2009).

10. "National Eating Disorders Screening Program," Screening for Mental
    Health, n.d., <http://www.mentalhealthscreening.org/events/nedsp/>
    (March 5, 2009).

11. "Amy's Story—Anorexia," adapted from *Girl's Life*, Home & Garden
    Publication, February, March, 2002. <http://findarticles.com/p/articles/
    mi_m0IBX/is_4_8/ai_82351530?tag=content;col1> (March 5, 2009).

12. Ibid.

13. Ibid.

14. Ibid.

15. Ibid.

16. Ibid.

17. "States for Treatment Access and Research Program (STAR)," National
    Eating Disorders Association, 2009, <http://www.nationaleatingdisorders.org/
    programs-events/star-program.php> (March 5, 2009).

18. Academy for Eating Disorders, "Worldwide Charter for Action on Eating
    Disorders," (updated August 2008), <http://www.aedweb.org/documents/
    WWCharter4.pdf> (March 5, 2009).

19. Daniel le Grange, PhD, and James Lock, MD, PhD, "Family-based
    Treatment of Adolescent Anorexia Nervosa: The Maudsley Approach,"
    Maudsley Parents, n.d., <http://www.maudsleyparents.org/
    whatismaudsley.html> (March 5, 2009).

20. Amanda-Jane Hazelwood, "Using text messaging in the treatment of eating
    disorders," *Nursing Times*, 104:40, pp. 28–29, <http://www.nursingtimes.net/
    printPage.html?pageid=1891029> (March 5, 2009).

21. "New Grants Will Further Understanding of the Biology, Genetics and Treatment of Eating Disorders," National Institute of Mental Health, September 23, 2008, <http://www.nimh.nih.gov/science-news/2008/new-grants-will-further-understanding-of-the-biology-genetics-and-treatment-of-eating-disorders.shtml> (March 5, 2009).

22. Daniel le Grange and Roslyn Binford Hopf, "ED Parent Support Project," The Eating Disorders Program at the University of Chicago Hospitals, n.d., <http://psychiatry.uchicago.edu/clinical/clinics/edp/> (March 5, 2009).

23. "Definition of bulimia susceptibility gene," MedicineNet.com, (reviewed January 19, 2003), <http://www.medterms.com/script/main/art.asp?articlekey=22184> (March 5, 2009).

24. "New Grants Will Further Understanding of the Biology, Genetics and Treatment of Eating Disorders."

25. "Impaired Brain Activity Underlies Impulsive Behaviors in Women with Bulimia," National Institute of Mental Health, January 12, 2009, <http://www.nimh.nih.gov/science-news/2009/impaired-brain-activity-underlies-impulsive-behaviors-in-women-with-bulimia.shtml> (March 5, 2009).

26. "Women Cannot Control Their Hunger As Well As Men, Study Shows," *Science Daily*, January 22, 2009, <http://www.sciencedaily.com/releases/2009/01/090121211340.htm> (March 5, 2009).

27. "Media Watchdog," National Eating Disorders Association, 2009, <http://www.nationaleatingdisorders.org/programs-events/media-watchdog.php> (March 5, 2009).

28. "Families do not cause anorexia nervosa," *Bio-medicine*, January 22, 2007, <http://news.bio-medicine.org/biology-news-3/Families-do-not-cause-anorexia-nervosa-3255-1/> (March 5, 2009).

Chapter 7: Living With Eating Disorders

1. RealMentalHealth.com, "Eating Disorders Treatment and Recovery: How Long Does It Take to Recover?" <http://www.realmentalhealth.com/eating__disorders/treatment_01_2.asp> (March 3, 2009).

2. Gurze Books, "Defining What It Means to Be 'Recovered,'" <http://www.gurze.com/client/client_pages/printable_pages/nl_edt_6_3pring.cfm> (March 3, 2009).

3. Ibid.

4. ABCNews.com, "Male Binge Eating: One Man's Courageous Story," Raina Seitel Gittlin, <http://abclocal.go.com/kgo/story?section=news/bizarre&id=5067605> (March 1, 2009).

5. Ibid.

6. CTV.ca, "Ex-Male Model Opens Up about Battle of the Binge," *Canadian Press*, July 21, 2007, <http://www.ctv.ca/servlet/ArticleNews/story/CTVNews/20070721/ron_saxen_070721/20070721> (March 1, 2009).

7. Ibid.

8. Gurze Books, "Relapse Prevention: Once Is Enough," <http:www.gurze.com/client/client_pages/nl_edt_5_2.cfm> (March 3, 2009).

9. S. Bauer, et al., "Use of Text Messaging in the Aftercare of Patients with Bulimia Nervosa," *European Eating Disorders Review*, Vol. 11, No. 3, pp. 279–290, published online April 25, 2003, Wiley InterScience, <http://www.interscience.wiley.com/journal/104528306/abstract?CRETRY=1&SRETRY=0> (March 4, 2009).

10. SomethingFishy.org, "Motivations for Recovery," <http://www.something-fishy.org/reach/motivations.php> (March 3, 2009).

11. SomethingFishy.org, "Coping Alternatives," <http://www.something-fishy.org/reach/waystocope.php#do> (March 3, 2009).

12. MayoClinic.com, "Bulimia Nervosa," <http://www.mayoclinic.com/print/bulimia/D500607/DSECTION=coping=and=support> (March 3, 2009).

13. MayoClinic.com, "Anorexia Nervosa," <http://www.mayoclinic.com/print/anorexia/DS00606/METHOD=print&DSECTION=all> (March 3, 2009).

14. National Eating Disorders Association, "Listen to Your Body," <http://www. nationaleatingdisorders.org/p.asp?WebPage_ID=320+Profile_ID=54933> (March 6, 2009).

15. MayoClinic.com, "Binge-Eating Disorder," <http://www.mayoclinic.com/print/binge-eating-disorder/DS00608/METHOD=print&DSECTION=tests-and-diagnosis#l> (March 3, 2009).

16. Carolyn Costin, *The Eating Disorder Sourcebook*, 3rd ed. (New York: McGraw Hill, 2007), pp. 91–97.

17. FertilityFactor.com, "Eating Disorders and Infertility," <http://www.fertilityfactor.com/infertility_female_infertility_eating_disorders.html.> (March 5, 2009).

18. Ibid.

19. MedicineNet.com, "Pregnancy Triggers Binge Eating in Some," WebMD Health News, Selma Boyles, September 7, 2007, <http://www.medicinenet.com/script/main/art.asp?articlekey=83775> (March 4, 2009).

Glossary

amenorrhea—The absence of menstruation; occurs in anorexia.

anemia—A shortage of red blood cells; can occur in anorexia.

anorexia nervosa—An eating disorder characterized by an obsession with thinness, starvation, weight less than 85 percent of normal, and amenorrhea in females. Binge eating and purging may also occur.

antidepressant—A drug taken to relieve depression; also used to treat eating disorders.

antiemetic—A drug that discourages vomiting; sometimes taken in the early stages of bulimia treatment.

anxiety—A medical condition marked by an intense fear of real or imagined danger.

binge-eating disorder—An eating disorder characterized by regularly eating huge amounts of food rapidly over a short time period, without purging.

body dysmorphic disorder—A chronic mental illness in which a person cannot stop thinking about a flaw in his or her appearance.

body mass index (BMI)—The most accurate measurement of overweight and obesity. BMI is calculated by dividing weight in pounds by height in inches squared and multiplying by 703. A BMI between 18.5 and 24.9 is considered normal.

bulimia nervosa—An eating disorder characterized by repeated binge eating and then various forms of purging.

cognitive behavioral therapy—A form of psychotherapy that emphasizes how a person's thinking influences his or her feelings and actions.

depression—A psychiatric disorder marked by feelings of hopelessness, dejection, lack of energy, and sleeplessness.

diabulimia—A disorder among people with diabetes in which they skip or restrict their insulin intake to lose weight.

dialectical behavioral therapy—A therapy that helps people validate their emotions and behaviors, examine those that negatively impact their lives, and try to bring about positive changes.

diuretic—A drug that increases urination; often abused by people with eating disorders to lose weight.

dopamine—A chemical that transmits messages between nerve cells in the brain.

eating disorders not otherwise specified (EDNOS)—A group of eating disorders that do not fit the criteria for anorexia nervosa or bulimia nervosa.

exercise disorder—A disorder in which people try to get rid of calories by excessively exercising for several hours every day. They may feel intense guilt or anxiety if they do not exercise.

family-based therapy—A therapy in which family members are directly involved in the patient's treatment and recovery process.

genetics—A branch of biology that deals with heredity.

hormones—Chemical substances made by the body that control the functioning of certain cells or organs.

human genome sequence—A map that shows all the genes in the human body in exact order.

incidence—The number of new cases of a disease diagnosed every year.

infertility—The inability to become pregnant.

interpersonal therapy—A therapy that deals with the connection between patients' symptoms and their relationship issues.

intuitive eating—Listening to and obeying the body's cues about hunger and fullness.

ipecac—A substance that causes vomiting and can damage the heart muscle.

lanugo—Fine hair that grows on the body of people with severe anorexia as protection from the cold, when there is not enough body fat for insulation.

laxative—A drug that causes bowel movements.

Maudsley Approach—Intensive outpatient therapies for eating disorders in which parents (or guardians) play an active and positive role in a patient's treatment and recovery.

neuroimaging—Using techniques such as MRIs and PET scans, to image the structure and function of the brain.

obesity—The condition of being extremely overweight.

obsessive-compulsive disorder—A disorder characterized by unwanted repetitive thoughts and behaviors.

osteoporosis—Thinning of bones and a decrease in bone mass density that makes people prone to fractures.

parity—Quality of status or position.

pica—An eating disorder that causes people to eat nonfood items.

predisposition—A tendency to develop a disease because of hereditary or other factor.

prevalence—The estimated number of people in a population who have a disease at a certain time.

psychotherapy—The treatment of a behavior disorder, mental illness, or any other condition by psychological means.

purging—Ridding the body of food by using laxatives or diuretics or inducing vomiting; also includes over-exercising to get rid of calories.

relapse—Reverting back to unhealthy behaviors, such as bingeing, purging, and starving after treatment.

risk—A condition, behavior, or other element that increases the chance of developing a disease.

serotonin—A chemical that transmits messages between nerve cells in the brain.

support group—An informal group where people with similar problems can meet, share ideas, and get support; not a substitute for professional therapy.

trigger—Something that can cause someone to develop an eating disorder; also, something that can cause someone with an eating disorder to starve, binge, or purge. It may be a stressful event, an object, a memory, or even a photo of a certain food item.

For More Information

Further Reading

Arnold, Carrie and B. Timothy Walsh. *Next to Nothing: A Firsthand Account of One Teenager's Experience with an Eating Disorder (Adolescent Mental Health Initiative)*. New York: Oxford University Press, 2007.

Benson, Lorri Antosz and Taryn Leigh Benson. *Distorted: How a Mother and Daughter Unraveled the Truth, the Lies, and the Realities of an Eating Disorder*. Deerfield Beach, Fla.: Health Communications, Inc., 2008.

Favor, Leslie J. *Weighing In: Nutrition and Weight Management*. New York: Marshall Cavendish, 2007.

Keel, Pamela. *Eating Disorders*. New York: Chelsea House Publishers: 2006.

Orr, Tamra. *When the Mirror Lies: Anorexia, Bulimia, and Other Eating Disorders*. Danbury, Conn.: Franklin Watts, 2007.

Sigler, Jamie-Lynn. *Wise Girl: What I've Learned About Life, Love, and Loss*. New York: Pocket Books, 2002.

Internet Addresses

American Psychiatric Association. HealthyMinds.org. © 2009.
<http://www.healthyminds.org/Main-Topic/Eating-Disorders.aspx>

National Eating Disorders Association. © 2009.
<http://www.nationaleatingdisorders.org/index.php>

Organizations

Academy for Eating Disorders
111 Deer Lake Road, Suite 100
Deerfield, IL 60015
(847) 498-4274
<http://www.aedweb.org>

American Dietetic Association
120 South Riverside Plaza, Suite 2000
Chicago, IL 60606
(800) 877-1600
<http://www.eatright.org/>

Eating Disorders Coalition for Research, Policy, and Action
720 7th Street NW, Suite 300
Washington, DC 20001
(202) 543-9570
<http://www.eatingdisorderscoalition.org>

National Association of Anorexia Nervosa and Associated Disorders
P.O. Box 7
Highland Park, IL 60035
(847) 831-3438
<http://www.anad.org>

National Eating Disorders Association
603 Stewart Street, Suite 803
Seattle, WA 98101
(206) 382-3587
<http://www.nationaleatingdisorders.org>

National Institute of Mental Health
Science Writing, Press, and Dissemination Branch
6001 Executive Boulevard, Room 8184, MSC 9663
Bethesda, MD 20892
(866) 615-6464 (toll-free)
<http://www.nimh.nih.gov/>

Overeaters Anonymous, Inc.
P.O. Box 44020
Rio Rancho, NM 87174
(505) 891-2664
<http://www.oa.org/>

Index

R

race(s), 10, 20, 40, 56, 82, 91, 107
recovery, 12, 17, 24, 79, 81, 88, 99, 102,
    107, 112, 120–123, 125, 128, 129, 131, 134
rehabilitation, 96
relapse(s), 50, 121, 125, 128–130
relaxing, 132
Renfrew Center Foundation for Eating
    Disorders, 19
restaurant(s), 21, 123, 134
restrict(ion), 32, 74, 93, 125, 135
risk, 10, 20, 57–59, 62, 68, 70, 71–77, 92,
    93, 104, 105, 114–116, 118, 119

S

seizures, 33, 93
self
    criticism, 75
    esteem, 8, 58, 68, 69, 75, 81, 127
    starvation, 49, 51
    worth, 32, 69, 79, 81, 121
serotonin, 73, 95
side effect(s), 50, 95, 98
Sigler, Jamie-Lynn, 11–16
sleep-eating disorder, 40, 41
States for Treatment, Access, and Research
    (STAR), 109
stomach pain, 23, 32, 33
stress(ful), 20, 22, 30, 37, 40, 58, 61, 65, 70,
    75, 96, 97, 100, 105, 121, 123–125, 127,
    129, 131, 134
suicide, 12, 52, 53, 70, 102
support groups, 103, 105, 113, 128
symptom(s), 8, 10, 18, 23, 26, 27, 39, 40,
    50, 51, 60, 75, 87, 90, 103, 113, 129

T

talk therapy, 98
teens, 15, 20, 21–23, 34, 57, 61, 64, 65,
    67–69, 73, 75, 77, 78, 84, 88, 93, 103, 110,
    112, 113, 135
television, 10, 11, 13, 43, 61, 62, 64
test(ing), 85, 87, 89, 91, 109, 112, 116

testosterone, 28, 92
therapist(s), 12, 14, 31, 43, 66, 80, 81, 83,
    85–89, 96, 98, 100, 102, 107, 111–113,
    120–123, 128–130, 132–135
thinness, 8, 27, 56, 61, 64, 72, 79
thyroid, 43, 52, 87
tooth decay, 23
Topamax, 93, 95
training, 103, 104
trauma, 70, 72, 115, 121, 128
treatment(s), 10, 14, 17, 18–21, 23, 24, 26,
    34, 39, 40, 49, 50, 60, 66, 79–91, 93–106,
    108–110, 112, 113, 118, 120, 121, 123,
    124, 128, 129, 134, 135

U

underweight, 15, 34, 99
University of Connecticut, 113
United States Census Bureau, 19
United States Department of Agriculture
    (USDA), 63, 76

V

vitamin(s), 92, 133
vomit(ing), 8, 10, 14, 18, 23, 24, 32–37,
    41–43, 45–47, 53, 55, 60, 62, 81, 82, 84,
    86, 89, 94, 125

W

Worldwide Charter for Action on Eating
    Disorders, 108, 109
Web sites, 113, 125, 131
weight
    gain, 8, 41, 93, 110
    loss, 14, 27, 41, 70, 93, 95, 96, 99, 100, 101, 106
wrestling, 23, 34

Y

yoga, 76, 118

Z

Zyprexa, 93